TO BE
FAIR

TO BE FAIR

Confessions of a District Court Judge

ROSEMARY RIDDELL

upstart press

A catalogue record for this book is available from the National Library of
New Zealand

ISBN 978-1-990003-16-5

An Upstart Press Book
Published in 2021 by Upstart Press Ltd
Level 6, BDO Tower, 19—21 Como St, Takapuna
Auckland 0622, New Zealand

Reprinted by Ligare, Auckland 2021

Designed by Nick Turzynski/Redinc. Book Design, www.redinc.co.nz
Printed by Everbest Printing Co. Ltd., China

Contents

For Mike

An' I will love thee still my dear
Till a' the seas gang dry

Preface

I HAD BEEN a judge for 12 years and after retiring from full-time work in December 2018 I took up an Acting Warrant. That enabled me to work part-time as a judge, travelling around the country on an as-needed basis. But just before this book was published, I relinquished my Acting Warrant.

This book represents many of the things I wanted to say at times, while on the bench. As you will see from some of the more ribald comments, it would never do for a *judge* to voice them. However, a retired judge can say what she likes, and there were, in my view, some things that needed to be said.

Put that together with the more personal reflections and here you have what I think on a number of topics. They are, of course, my own views and I don't expect everyone to agree with them. It would be a dreary old world indeed if we all thought the same.

Some of my colleagues may grumble that I have given away too much. That judging is such a high profession and it is impolite at best to divulge the more crass aspects of the job. They may be right.

On the other hand, I relate what actually happens. Any judge could add their own book of the humour and pathos that make up a judge's day. It really is that funny and that sad.

Writing the book has been a kind of therapy for me. I loved the job. I was very reluctant to let it go, but the amount of travel involved made it impractical. Then my now 92-year-old mother moved next door, at our invitation I should add.

I recognised a freedom in being available for coffees, taking long walks in the Ida Valley where we live and making time for playing the piano. I have a little chapel in our back garden. It is a perfect spot for reading and reflection. I wanted to make that part of the rhythm of my life too.

Then, of course, there's Mike, my partner of 46 years. It was my idea to live in Central Otago in the first place. I figured the endless sky, and all that fresh air, might chase away his prostate cancer. He has always loved Central and that love is shared by our daughter and son-in-law who now live just 50 metres down the road.

I realised there are things you must let go. Knowing that meant my job, I started, on a whim, writing about it one day and couldn't stop. I wanted to tell the stories of those in both the Family Court and the criminal jurisdiction where I worked. I wanted to draw attention to their struggles and triumphs.

I also wanted people to see that judges are not high and mighty or unreachable. We are just ordinary people doing a rather demanding and difficult job, and it is a job that keeps our feet on the ground.

I don't apologise for the language you'll find here. If your sensibilities are offended, then maybe this is not for you. But I figure it is okay. In many cases I have faithfully repeated what people have said, and I did want to be an honest recorder of the facts! Moreover, it is hard to watch a movie, peruse Facebook or overhear a conversation these days without a few expletives being dotted about. To that extent, we are blasé about it.

We used to tell our children it was okay to swear, provided you saved it for stuff like banging your thumb with a hammer. So the odd swear word was never entirely taboo when the children were growing up.

I realise I wander in the book from tales of judging to other subjects, on which I am certainly not an expert. But to the extent we are all living in Aotearoa New Zealand, we all have views about those thorny issues of poverty, family violence and racism. I have put in my two cents' worth. They are views that have been influenced by my years on the bench and coloured by what I have observed.

The other aspect of this story that is perhaps surprising for some is the personal one. Mike and I have known grief, like many. I have found time and time again that sharing that grief can be healing for the listener. It leads to other stories being shared and so breaks through the barrier of keeping pain buried deep.

My parents lost their first child only days after she was born healthy in 1951. Thereafter no one spoke of it. Not my parents' families, not friends. No one. I realise we have come some way since then, but still we bottle up stuff and it spews out in all kinds of inappropriate ways. What if we could be honest about our pain?

At the other end of the spectrum there's humour, and I am a firm believer that we all need a healthy dose of it on a regular basis. Sometimes, it has been difficult being a judge, and I have wanted to stuff my gown in my mouth to stop from laughing helplessly at what goes on. Especially when a witness or defendant is completely oblivious to the effect of what they have just said.

They say, 'sober as a judge', which I gather has nothing to do with alcohol intake but is more about a serious, grave manner. It is that image I wanted to poke a few holes in.

My children call me Judge Mental. It is an indication of the lack of deference shown me at home. They have kept me honest in a job where it is tempting to believe your own myths, namely that you hold the power, and all others must defer to you. In fact, we judges are servants of the people. We are here to carry out the legislative decisions and statutes enacted by Parliament. We cannot make up our own idea of justice, nor can we impose some random sentence on a hapless defendant just because we don't like the cut of their jib. Our role is to treat everyone the same, with impartiality and respect.

That said, we are human — very human — and in the pages that follow you will see exactly what I mean.

Enjoy!

1 Mental health

'YOU SEE JUDGE, I don't need to be in hospital. I'm feeling fine. I've got somewhere to stay.'

It all sounded plausible. If I'd asked him to stop there, he might have been discharged. But I'd read the file: paranoid delusions, frequent hospitalisations. The medical team were united in their view he should remain on the ward.

'And I've got money.'

'Oh, yes?' I said. 'Tell me about that.'

'Well, last week I won two trillion on Lotto. Don't tell anyone — especially not those people sitting behind you.'

Where? I almost turned round, then remembered the bare wall behind me.

''Cause they're ready to rip me off.'

'Okay, sir. Thank you. I'm going to make a decision.'

I can see the medical team are relieved. They know what's coming.

'Sir, I think it's great you're feeling better and have organised some digs. I know you're anxious to leave hospital, but I think it's a bit early in your recovery.'

I expect an outburst. Instead, he pulls his hat on, says, 'Yeah, I expected that,' and shuffles out with a wink to the security guard.

Every time they go, every time I think it could be me. The circuitry in the brain gone awry, a head injury or a cataclysmic life event from which there's no coming back.

A university student struck down with schizophrenia, a talented saxophone player kicked unconscious outside a bar and left unable to speak, let alone play.

My unending fascination with law is the parade of humanity, people's stories, the way a single event can irretrievably change a life. One minute a businessman, the next a psych patient. With that transition comes a new way of being viewed, in the street, on TV, in the media, by the court system.

Sometimes, not always, it's obvious. There's the twitch or constant jiggle, a side-effect of medication, mismatched clothes, the unnerving fixed stare.

The compliant ones agree to stay in hospital. They are usually in the minority. The spirited mount a defence, write long letters with diagrams and spaceship illustrations. They speak with passion. They know their words are futile, but sometimes they strike a small victory.

One of my colleagues, after listening carefully, nodding, delivers the bad news. 'I'm sorry, you need to remain in hospital. Now is there anything else you want to say?'

'No, you short, fat, bald bastard.'

A nurse in the back row is heard to mumble, 'Well, at least there's nothing wrong with his eyesight.'

That same judge recalls another occasion when the patient refused to come into the courtroom. So, judge, registrar, security officer, doctor and nurse joined her in the lounge for the hearing. The judge sat next to her on one side with the psychiatric nurse on the other. His Honour started explaining who he was and what the hearing was all about. He asked if there was anything she wanted to tell him.

She sat there for a moment and then leaned towards the nurse and said, 'Can you please tell him to fuck off!'

The said judge commiserated with himself that at least she didn't call him fat.

I have to be on guard. Long explanations about how a person came to be brought to hospital can be believable.

Sure, the wife can be irritating and you may want to retaliate. Gluing the toilet seat down and putting the dining room chairs up a tree could be an expression of frustration in a marriage. It's not how I'd express myself, but who's to say?

I discharge him, partly because he acknowledges his behaviour is a bit wacky but promises to find more reasonable outlets for his frustration in future.

All good. On my next visit to the hospital, he's back. Seems I'd underestimated his knack for annoying his wife. This time, he'd glued all the doors shut, including cupboards, the shower door and, with what was left of the glue, every pair of his wife's shoes to the floor of the wardrobe.

How do we judges assess when odd behaviour slips into madness? It might be unusual to choose to hang out the washing in the nude, or a tad antisocial to insist on walking backwards and then berate people you bump into. But behaviour is only part of the story.

A person's mental health history and the observations of family, friends and neighbours can be telling. The size of a file is often a giveaway.

When the first diagnosis was 20 years ago and there have been regular admissions to hospital ever since, a mental disorder can be entrenched and difficult to treat.

After all, who wants to be on medication that will see you put on 20 kilos or start trembling uncontrollably? And so the rhythm of life goes like this. Get hospitalised. Take the meds, feel clearer but struggle with the side-effects. Stop the meds. Stay away from mental health services. Get sick. Yell at all the voices in your head, and this antisocial behaviour sees you brought back to hospital by police. And so back to meds.

If I've learned anything from my visits to various psychiatric hospitals, it's that this arm of medicine is probably the least certain of the sickness, treatment, wellness scenario of other branches.

The brain is a unique and wonderful organ, but two people can have the same mental disorder, be treated with the same medication, and react so differently. Maybe clozapine will do the trick. If not, we'll try risperidone or olanzapine.

Small wonder patients come to court loudly proclaiming their refusal to take any medication.

'Do you know what it's like?' one middle-aged lady demanded, pointing her finger at me and clutching a very large bag. 'I can't knit any more. I just can't concentrate.' She jerks open the bag and multicoloured balls of wool bounce everywhere. Suddenly there are bobbing heads under the table as doctor and nurses try to retrieve the escaping balls. 'My life is over. And it's all *your* fault.'

Indeed, it is. She needs someone to focus her anger and despair on, to assure herself it's not her brain but that toffee-nosed woman in front of her — who doesn't look like she could knit anyway!

Unlike the family or criminal court, however, where the buck stops with me, there is an escape hatch. I'm grateful to the doctor, his arms full of wool, who takes it from here. 'Well, we could have a discussion back on the ward about different meds. I'm sure there's something that won't impede her concentration to the same degree.'

I think to myself maybe *he* could take up knitting with all that wool. 'Behave,' says my adult to my very erring child.

It's not uncommon for patients and doctors to be accompanied by supporters to a hearing. One psychiatrist always brings his dog Wilson, a small, well-behaved creature, whom I'm told settles people on a ward. 'He has a soothing influence that's quite surprising if there's some conflict between patients,' his owner proudly notes.

One day an outpatient arrived at court ready for her hearing with what looked suspiciously like a pair of ears poking out of her shopping bag. As it turned out, her rabbit went everywhere with her and, when I returned to court to recount this tale to the other judges, they were way ahead of me. 'Oh yes, we've met Lester. He poops a lot.'

Probably the most unusual accompaniment I ever encountered was the man who ushered in his three sisters and a pet pony. His diagnosis was delusional behaviour. As the only child of two quiet, patient-looking elderly folk, his condition was entrenched and hard to treat. One had to give him a wide berth to make way for the invisible pony.

Years ago, I was involved in a church, Ponsonby Baptist, that welcomed those with mental disorders. The psych community, as they were then known, lived in local boarding houses. They were never going to get 'well', but their insights and straightforward leave-the-social-niceties-at-home manner taught us so much. Each Christmas we would visit all of the boarding houses with an ice-cream container full of such essentials as a pack of smokes, comb, soap and a $20 note. Our children enjoyed the experience and knew they didn't get to open their own presents until after we'd been to the boarding houses. I think they learned to respect those who seemed different.

In 1991 after the government's budget cuts eviscerated welfare benefits, we held a party for all those affected. It was a way of giving the finger to those who thought such people could somehow manage with less when life was already challenging enough.

Those who participated in the life of the church came to expect there would be some unusual occurrences, especially when people were particularly manic. At morning tea one Sunday, a gentleman singled out my husband Mike and asked him fervently, 'You're like me Mike, you're like me. Have you had a brain injury?'

Mike was the minister of the church at the time and had come to expect interruptions during the service, like the time he posed a rhetorical question: 'And what's safe sex anyway?' Came the reply from the back, 'It's sex with a condom on, Mike.' That was Tania, an affable young woman.

We once arranged a birthday party for another character,

Maryanne, at her place, arriving with cake, food and presents. The food was eaten pretty quickly and then as we were settling down, Maryanne announced, 'You'll have to go. I'm off to town.' Off we went, laughing among ourselves at the way she'd dispatched us, minus the etiquette.

Some make a stab at the polite society lingo. A friend gave $20 to someone on Ponsonby Road one day. 'Thanks very much,' he said. 'We must do lunch sometime.'

From the experience of working alongside those with mental illness came *The Insatiable Moon*, a feature-length film I directed, written by my husband, centring on one such boarding house. But that's another story.

Not all judges enjoy doing mental health work. Some find the confrontational nature of the work and the anguish of those struggling with a mental disorder too much. Moreover, in a hospital courtroom, the judge sits much closer to the medical team and parties. It can be unnerving when a patient stares unblinkingly at you throughout the hearing from only a couple of metres away. The traditional courtroom provides a greater physical distance, which can be comforting.

Then there are judges who do enjoy the work but who can leave the patient very confused. One gentleman told the judge he wanted to get back home for his 'calving'. The judge was interested and enquired whether he worked in wood or stone.

Sometimes it's the patient who can unravel the judge. Like the prostitute with mental health issues who arrived at court clutching a large diary. While the judge was doing his introductory remarks, she interrupted with, 'You look like a bit of a goer. I've got a gap at two o'clock tomorrow.'

I'm always impressed by those who choose to make mental health their area of expertise, whether that be doctor, nurse or community worker. They are well used to crazy behaviour. They don't snigger or raise their eyebrows. Theirs is not a sexy field of medicine, but by and large they exhibit a degree of kindness which is humbling to observe.

In a hearing, a patient may deliver a rant about the psychiatrist whom they dislike, say, because they're black. The doctor sits there quite unperturbed. Or, in one case the doctor was American and I was given a lengthy explanation about how the patient was sure this doctor was a first cousin of Trump and how *that* was enough grounds for her to refuse any treatment of any kind. I know the medical people are trained to take these responses in their stride, but I have a sneaking admiration for their unflappability in these unusual circumstances.

The judge must remain imperturbable despite interjections and complaints. One patient moaned he wasn't happy with the judge in front of him. 'I want a *real* judge, one of those High Court judges. They're the real deal.'

'Well,' said our unruffled judge, 'there are a lot of people, including me, who think I *should* be on the High Court, but you'll just have to put up with me today.'

In all mental health hearings, I am accompanied by a security guard and a court registrar. The former is all togged up in his safety gear, and despite his best efforts can look quite intimidating. Those patients who've experienced the criminal jurisdiction sometimes recognise the security guard and strike up a conversation with them or just glare.

Patients mistake the registrar for the judge and look surprised when I introduce myself. Some comment on my clothes. We don't wear gowns in mental health hearings. I remember one psychiatrist who always made a point of checking out my shoes. If they reached her high standard, she would give me a thumbs up as she left the court.

In the main, patients are represented by their own lawyers, unless they specifically decline one, in which case the district inspector will sit in on the hearing to make sure the patient's rights are observed.

Lawyers have a difficult job, to take their client's instructions and convey them to the judge. Difficult if your client insists on letting the judge know what are actually their delusions, not facts. A lawyer needs to be canny and compassionate all at once. Like the doctors, it's the lawyers who enjoy this kind of work who usually end up acting for people. Which is a relief, because you don't want some lawyer who is hell bound on telling the judge *exactly* what their client's instructions were.

If the lawyers need to be sensitive, families do too. Those who live with a family member who has a mental disorder have a challenging and full-time commitment. One father, whose son ran amok in the courtroom and had to be removed, sat quietly through it all. When asked if he had expected the outburst, he said no, his son had been quite calm on the way over, although they did have to stop en route so his son could hug some trees.

The Mental Health (Compulsory Assessment and Treatment) Act was passed in 1992 and provides a legal framework for those who need treatment for a mental disorder. The act also endeavours to safeguard patient rights. For example, a judge must always see a patient, even in a lock-up ward. It's not enough to be told the person is unwell and can't come to court. In those instances, the court must go to them. A conversation may not be possible with someone crouched near naked in a corner, but generally a judge must introduce themselves and have a kōrero with the person before hearing the evidence elsewhere.

There are two main orders for which an application may be made. The first is an Inpatient Order where a person needs to be hospitalised on the grounds that either: they pose a serious danger to their health and safety or that of others; or they have a seriously diminished capacity to take care of themselves.

The second one is a Community Order where someone doesn't need hospital treatment but must agree to take medication and treatment as prescribed.

Both orders last for up to six months and then lapse or

can be extended and subsequently have effect indefinitely.

Sometimes a patient will challenge their hospitalisation under section 16 of the Mental Health Act. That requires a review of the patient's status, whereby a hearing occurs 'as soon as practicable', but in any event should be within days. It's often at the point where a person has developed some insight into their illness and wants to go home, or to feed the cat, or pay the mortgage, or because they find the hospital environment difficult. Those are all plausible reasons.

The judge must balance the patient request with the available medical evidence. Are they ready to be discharged? Will they comply with treatment in the community? Or is the court setting them up for failure with a premature clearance?

It can be an enormously difficult decision.

The forensic ward can be challenging. That is where patients are held if they are unfit to stand trial because they are mentally unwell or have been sentenced for an offence and removed from the prison to the hospital because of a mental disorder. Security is tighter and so getting in and out of these wards is more of a rigmarole, and rightly so. Although, at one hospital we went through the first set of doors, were handed our duress alarms, locked in the next section and left there. Either someone went to lunch and forgot about us or thought the judge and her registrar would benefit from a wee stay in the forensic unit.

I would have thought that someone who has been moved from prison to a ward would be happy to stay there. It seems to me to be a brighter and more congenial atmosphere than the jail setting. Yet, many patients are very keen to get back to prison. Their attempts at lucidity are not always successful, but they try, not realising their words unstitch them.

Others might be in the ward for serious offending, such as murder, and, occasionally as their mental state improves, they develop more insight about what they did and how it impacted on the victim's family. Sometimes they have killed a wife or daughter. Those who have come to understand they have taken a life are deeply remorseful and contrite, although it's not for me to consider discharging them from hospital. In the forensic ward, I am only required to either make another Inpatient Order, requiring them to stay in hospital, or alternatively discharge them back to prison.

On the ward, there is a greater security presence. Occasionally I am given orders about how and when to leave if things unravel. Three beefy nurses arrive first, followed by the doctor and nurse. I am invariably surprised to see a weedy-looking individual follow, who looks as if he couldn't take down his granny, never mind a judge. Still, first impressions can be deceptive.

I remember on one occasion waiting for everyone to arrive and take their seats. As always, I addressed the patient first, introducing myself and asking if he knew why he was here. He, a gentleman in knee-high socks, open-toed sandals and somewhat strange handknitted jersey, duly informed me he was the psychiatrist.

I have always found mental health hearings to be full of surprises, with a dash of pathos and a splash of humour.

The men and women who strive to live a life that's as normal as they can make it in the face of what is sometimes a debilitating illness have my deepest respect for their courage.

Who would choose this particular form of affliction?

Would I manage any better?

2 Judicial camaraderie

WHEN I'M APPOINTED as a judge in 2006, one of the first and most memorable impressions is the depth of support I receive from other judges. Almost all of them are strangers to me, apart from those in the city where I practised law, but I receive phone calls, emails and texts, cards, and lunch and dinner invitations.

I am also accorded an honour, not offered to everyone. The local kaumātua offers to bless my chambers. It's a brief ceremony but charged with atmosphere, with wairua.

There is an unwritten law that judges never occupy another judge's courtroom, so no sitting in the back row to check out another's performance. That law extends to no criticism of another colleague's judgment, no matter how harsh or light it may seem. We all know there's far more to sentencing than the piecemeal offering dribbled to the public via the media. We know from our own sentencing efforts how fraught that exercise can be.

For a newbie judge, it's all very mesmerising and comforting too when others recall their tales of initiation to the bench. One tells me of getting his gown caught on the leg of his chair and disappearing, like a magician, under the bench. Another accidentally pushes the panic button, which brings police and security bursting into his courtroom.

Where to sit when you enter a strange courtroom can be testing. One judge entered, then had a tussle with the registrar as the judge tried to sit on her seat. The registrar gave the judge a withering look and, with very sharp elbows, banished the hapless judge to her place higher up, much to the amusement of the local lawyers.

Then another shamefacedly recalls how she waited for all to stand at the commencement of court. One errant person remained seated. She started to upbraid him, before noticing the arm of his wheelchair.

That same judge developed a reputation for preferring a very low temperature in the courtroom, leaving the lawyers shivering. Truth was, she was going through menopause and found the heavy black gown unbearable at times. One day a woman came to court having breached her sentence. 'So why didn't you do your community work?' asked the judge.

'I can't 'cause I'm going through menopause.'

Wrong judge to try that excuse on. She replied, 'I am too, and I can get to work every day.' One hundred hours' community work was added to the sentence.

Still another remembers being a new judge in court with a room full of lawyers. The court was hushed. The judge heard a distinctive bird call. She had recently moved from the South to the North Island and, knowing the bird calls were different, asked in her best judicial voice whether anyone could enlighten her as to that particular bird call. Senior counsel informed her it was a car alarm.

Such stories are, for me, very comforting. I know I'm going to make a dick of myself. It's just a question of when and how badly. But I'll be in good company. Yes, we can all be dicks at times.

I've never understood why the court day is organised with all judges having a cuppa at 9.45 before court starts at 10 a.m. and then another break at 11.30. Those with weak bladders, and that's most of us, as we are no spring chickens, have to allow for loo stops when we can. However, a judge can make a pronouncement, 'I'll take a short adjournment now to consider matters', if caught short.

Pace yourself, they tell me. The job is more demanding than you think. At the beginning, I'm still wondering how I'm going to manage to use the generous holidays allowed. It isn't too long before I realise every holiday is essential to balance out the peculiar pressures of this job.

Not a few judges come down with some ailment or other in their first few years of judicial life. For me it was a painful dose of shingles, another developed Bell's palsy, while yet another colleague suffered a sudden detached retina. We all know about the need for a work–life balance. It's a great idea, but, as they say, a half-baked idea is okay as long as it's in the oven.

We all know the work has to be taken home; evenings and weekends are often spent reading files for sentencing or trawling over the transcript of a trial. That's no different from life as a lawyer, except for a couple of vital differences. In my office, known as chambers, the phone almost never rings — twice a week if I'm lucky — and there are no time sheets to fill in, recording six-minute billings of chargeable work.

Indeed, one of the most satisfying aspects is the equitable nature of the job. We are all paid the same, from the newly appointed judge to the one who has been on the bench for over 20 years.

We've hit the proverbial glass ceiling. There's no promotion unless you aim for the dizzy heights of the High Court. We're all in this together, no one better than another, each happy to share their challenges and failures. Our common room consists of about a dozen judges. In the smaller centres there might be only one or two. Auckland boasts 30 or more.

I like the camaraderie of our common room. I like the dark humour, the slightly off-colour jokes and the self-deprecating wit. No one takes themselves too seriously. Law might be a serious business, but our shared humanity demands we poke the borax at each other, lest any pomposity arises.

I am among friends and deeply grateful. There will come a time when tragedy intrudes into our family. Our daughter dies. So many of them travel to Dunedin for her funeral. That includes our chief judge and those from both the North and South Islands. I'm told to take all the time I need to gather myself before I'm ready to return to work. Their messages tell me I am thought of and supported. I feel a wave of aroha surrounding Mike and me and our family.

When Mike develops prostate cancer, I need to be with him for the aftermath of the operation, and for those ongoing appointments when it's clear the cancer has spread. I tell my male colleagues they'd better get tested. Ribald jokes involving rubber gloves follow. They look bashful at the same time.

We share stories of our day. The effect of seeing one of our number on the bench is too much for one defendant about to be sentenced and he vomits everywhere. 'Was it something I said?' wonders the judge.

They're on a roll now. One judge remembers having to shoo away an elderly juror who set off to sit by him when his name was called. That same judge also recalls the juror who failed to turn up for the trial. When the registrar phoned him, the juror said he was in Auckland and suggested the judge get someone to sit in for him until he could make it the following day. When told the judge had fined another juror $200 for being absent, the recalcitrant juror said, 'Okay, I'll pay my mate $100 to drive me there today. Would that work?' Indeed, it did.

What about the witness who arrived in court to give evidence, stared hard at the bench and demanded: 'Who are *you*?'

Or the colleague who visited a tough area for the first

time, where the court was full of gang members. The first defendant had been charged with driving while disqualified, his twentieth offence. The judge assumed his sternest look and said, 'Where I come from, you'd be looking at a lengthy term of imprisonment for this, particularly given your extensive criminal history.'

A voice from the back of the courtroom called out, 'Yeah, well you can fuck off to where you came from then.'

These yarns remind us we're not held in universal regard, which also reminds me of the story about the man who waited hours in court for his minor traffic infringement to be heard. When he was finally called, he was told he'd have to wait until the next day. 'What for?' he snapped at the judge.

His Honour roared back, 'Twenty dollars for contempt of court. That's why.'

Noticing the man checking his wallet, the judge said, 'It's okay. You don't have to pay now.'

The man replied, 'I'm just seeing if I have enough for two more words.'

Early on, I attempt to accommodate parties by suggesting we hold hearings on my reserve day, which is kept free from court fixtures for writing decisions. I am blind to the reality, which is that a courtroom has to be found, together with a registrar, and a stenographer to type up the proceedings. Not for nothing are there rosters for judges' work and available courtrooms, which run months into the future.

There are also consequences for running a hearing late into the evening, which means a lot of people are affected. On one occasion, I had a Family Court fixture. It was scheduled to take a day. I could see the finish line. I asked if anyone minded if we kept going. There is probably not a lawyer or court staff in the land who would say no, unless there were urgencies like child minding and, even then, there are hurried texts to sort that out. So on we went to the bitter end. I asked the court stenographer to type up the final parenting order, so it could be stamped. That was done. All finished.

By this time, the cleaners were periodically hovering outside with their buckets and mops. It was after 7 p.m. and everyone staggered out of the courtroom. I made the brave offer to drive any of the staff home. The stenographer accepted, so we wound our way through the countryside to parts I had never been to before. I managed to get lost returning home. There's a moral here, but I think you get the picture.

In our common room, we have a fierce debate about whether children should be allowed to stay and watch court proceedings. A crying baby is a distraction, but Mum can't get a babysitter and this is a rare chance to see her partner, even if he is in the dock. A ban on children in court can only apply to that judge's courtroom. When a judge talks about 'my' courtroom, it's not just a possessive pronoun. It is their courtroom, to run as the judge chooses. So, we agree that if a particular judge isn't happy with young children in court, a notice will have to go on the courtroom door to that effect.

Outside the courtroom, we are more relaxed. Dinners are shared, jovial and sometimes raucous affairs.

One surprises me by telling me of his lifelong love of heavy metal, not exactly in accord with his persona. Another plays drums and has done so for years. Our music tastes are similar; well, except for the heavy metal head. Leonard Cohen and Van Morrison are favourites.

So why did I think all judges would be classical nuts?

The feeling of camaraderie extends beyond our common room. Around the country are judges I can call on for advice and mentoring. When I am appointed, I am also given a mentor, a senior fellow judge who can answer all the dumb questions without calling them dumb. They are just a phone call away and that's extraordinarily helpful.

We meet at seminars during the year, usually held in Wellington or Auckland and designed to upskill us on various topics pertinent to our job. It's a chance to catch up and chew the fat, to share war stories and memorable things people have said in court. Like the defendant leaving the dock who says cheerily to the judge 'See you later alligator', only to have the judge reply, 'At the trial crocodile.'

Such quick wit is not expected from the bench. We're meant to be old and stuffy, or at least perceived as that. But we remember judges of old, now no longer with us, who were quick with the jocular comment. Judge Mick Brown was one such judge. A lawyer was addressing the judge when a pager went off in his pocket. 'Mr X, I think your eggs are ready.'

The late Justice Fogarty, a respected judge of the High Court who retired in 2017, was asked what human quality he admired the most. He said, 'Humour — it binds us together. I find it very difficult sometimes to restrain myself on the bench.'[1]

That said, the same judge was once known to choke up while sentencing a man on fraud charges. He said, 'The Chinese community, particularly in this city, has its origins in the goldfields — in the same way that my family did. It's extremely rare to see a Chinese person from Otago before this court and it's most upsetting.'[2]

That blend of humour and compassion is what I aim for. It seems like a good goal.

It's rare for us all to be in the common room at the same time. Some judges are working elsewhere, others are on holiday. We have visiting judges, brought in occasionally if there's a conflict of interest for a local judge. Some of them get our humour, others don't. Some are judges with an Acting Warrant, judges who've retired and now work part-time wherever the work takes them. A kind of 'have gavel will travel'. They have a good fund of stories; sadly, many of them are unprintable.

And so, a year after my appointment, I'm reflecting one day in my chambers on the job. Would I go back to the practice of law? Never. Do I miss the cut and thrust of cross-examination? Sometimes. Is this what I was born to do? Absolutely. And I'm guided by that saying, 'I can and I will.' Watch me.

3 Sentencing

THE DEFENDANT WAS standing in the dock about to be sentenced on his twelfth burglary. The judge cleared his throat and leaned forward in his seat, then thundered, 'Twenty years!'

The defendant promptly fainted.

After he was revived, the judge continued, 'Twenty years — that's what you'll get if you're back in this court again.'

It's a complicated exercise when a defendant pleads guilty to a crime. The first question is whether they and the victim should attend a restorative justice conference, intended to confront the offender with the consequences of their crime and learn the impact of that on the victim. Such a step is mandatory, unless it's inappropriate, where domestic violence is involved or the victim declines to attend.

Thereafter, the Probation Service prepares a report which addresses the nature of the offending, the offender's background, work record, likelihood of reoffending, and remorse.

The judge will also receive any letters of support from family or employer. Sometimes the letter is from the defendant expressing remorse and promising to go straight from here on. I remember one letter in which the defendant agreed he had been '95 per cent' guilty of the offence, which he had crossed out and replaced by '60 per cent'. I took that remorse with a grain of salt.

Other letters of remorse are penned from prison with help from inmates who know the drill. The 'I've turned my life around, found religion, want to go straight, so give me another chance' lines are familiar. It needs a deft touch to determine whether these are the heartfelt words of a genuinely sorry defendant or are inspired by someone already doing a long lag.

The police may decide to weigh in with submissions on sentencing and, of course, the defendant's own lawyer may also file submissions seeking leniency and asking the court to take certain factors into account — for example, an impending birth of a baby, a family member's terminal illness, the offer of reparation, or the lack of previous offending. The birth of a baby is not uncommon — I mean in sentencing submissions, and I'm tempted to ask why the defendant didn't think of baby on the way when they were out stealing cars.

The scales of justice lean one way in favour of punishment, then the other in favour of compassion. In this case, punishment wins out, but I often hear that voice in my head, 'Mercy sister, mercy.'

Some judges may comment on the quality of particular offending. Take the solicitor whose male client was appearing in court on a charge of burglary with a co-accused female. The client was there, but the co-accused was nowhere to be seen. The lawyer told the judge, 'Your Honour, this is a case of chivalry. My client is going to take the rap on this matter. He has never offended before and he is an aspiring writer.'

Said the judge to the defendant, 'Well, considering this is your first offence, I don't think you have a blossoming career as a criminal. Maybe you'll fare better as a writer.'

The range of sentences that a judge can impose can vary from a discharge without conviction whereby a defendant walks free from the courtroom, through to a fine, community work, to home detention, or prison.

Four hundred hours of community work is the maximum allowable by law, with 40 hours as the minimum.

Twelve months' home detention is the maximum. Any home detention sentence requires a person to live at their home and generally remain there for the duration of the sentence.

Personally, I'd think that was a holiday, not a sentence.

While it sounds easy enough, though, it proves to be surprisingly hard, and many return to court before the sentence has been completed, having breached the conditions of home detention or asking for an alternative. Home detention is contrasted with community detention, which involves an overnight curfew.

'So how do I know whether 110 hours or 120 hours of community work is the correct sentence?' was my question to my colleagues early on. I hadn't worked in criminal law for seven years before my appointment, so getting it right was a challenge. Sometimes I could tell from a defendant's surprised look that I'd probably pitched it too high — or too low — based on what their lawyer had told them to expect beforehand. Years of training and the practice of law may have given me knowledge, but as the old saying goes, 'Knowledge is knowing tomato is a fruit. Wisdom is knowing not to put it in a fruit salad.' And wisdom comes with time.

Others would pay scant attention to my sentencing speech, knowing they would be going to prison for a raft of offences and waiting only for the magic word 'cumulative' or preferably 'concurrent'. The former meant the prison term of, say, six months was added to the rest of the sentence. Concurrent meant it was to be served at the same time.

Some sob in the dock as I speak. Others adopt a staunch 'I don't give a fuck' persona. Often a defendant would want to add to what their lawyer has said on their behalf as if they could do the job better.

Some bring their mates along thinking their friends'

gung-ho presence might add to their stature. That proved
to be sadly mistaken in one case.

The defendant was in custody. His bogan mates were in
the public gallery. Bogan defendant strutted out to plead
guilty to all charges. They were read out one by one. Assault
with a deadly weapon. 'Guilty.'

From the public gallery came 'Yeah', 'Go man', 'Cool'.

The second charge was assault using a brick as a weapon.
'Guilty.' Same response from the back row.

The third charge, assault using a crowbar. 'Guilty.' More
'ye haws' and endorsements.

Unfortunately, the defendant had failed to inform his
cobbers of the last charge. It was duly read: 'Indecent
relationship with a goat.'

'Guilty' from the shamefaced defendant.

'Yuk', 'Eeww', 'Gross' from the gallery and the bogans
bolted en masse.

There's a postscript to that story. In the afternoon,
court resumed and the court taker (who assists the judge
in running the court) made the usual call, 'All stand for His
Honour the judge', then more quietly as he was ascending
the stair came a goat-like 'Mee-hh'. The judge dissolved and
bolted like the bogans.

That same judge seemed to have an affinity for such
cases. He was once presiding over a judge-alone trial, a
charge of bestiality. In pre-trial directions, he said to the
assembled lawyers, 'We'll need to corral the witnesses,' then
realised his unfortunate choice of words.

It's not unusual for a defendant to arrive for sentencing
toting a gym bag. I wonder whether they're off to do
weights when I'm done or, more likely, they have their
toothbrush and PJs packed and ready on the advice of
their lawyer.

I ask Māori defendants if they feel whakamā, shame.
They nod, head bowed. I think the saddest thing is a young
person, up for sentencing, with no family support, lost, cast

adrift from whānau. I would ask those Māori who they were, where they were from.

We all have a need to belong, to have a place we can call home, to love and be loved. Never mind climbing the ladder of success. Some never even find the ladder.

To be unable to read and write is a terrible scourge on our society. How it happens for a child moved from pillar to post, never settling at one school long enough to learn, struggling with glue ear, eyesight difficulties or dyslexia is one thing. But that child grows into an adult, ill-equipped to fit into our society.

The brain of an 18-year-old is not yet fully developed. Those who've grown up in a dysfunctional home don't learn boundaries, or discipline, or consequences.

I try to explain to a young man I was sentencing for a number of burglaries what his theft meant to a family who lost irretrievable items, photos on a laptop, war medals and children's treasured toys.

'Would you feel stink if someone just took your stuff?' I asked.

'Yeah, I guess,' he grudgingly agreed.

I had one trial in which the father was charged with burglary after going to a farmhouse and, among other things, emptying all the children's drawers of their clothes. Not a smart move as he gave the clothes to his kids who wore them to school and, you guessed it, the children who'd been robbed recognised their hoodies and jeans. Some offenders don't think beyond the immediate action of the crime. That's probably why so many offenders are caught. I don't mean to diminish police skills of detection, but some make their job very easy.

I sentenced that same offender to a period of imprisonment and declined to take into account his plea that he 'did it for the kids'.

Some squirm in the dock as I go through an exercise which is as much for the higher court's benefit as for him. I need to demonstrate, in the event of an appeal, that I have carefully incorporated the law and referred to it. The Sentencing Act obliges me to denounce his conduct and hold him accountable, terms that are a mystery to him, so I try to translate. 'You've done a bad thing. You must now pay the price.'

I must refer to other leading cases involving similar offending to show I'm aware of, and have taken their tariff for offending, into account. I read the victim impact statement or let the victim speak. Either way, it's a poignant reminder of the cost of the offending when the victim puts it in their own words what they have suffered and the ongoing consequences of physical pain, loss or financial hardship.

I'm mindful of the press and watch as they pick up on a particular phrase, knowing that will go in the brief report in tomorrow's paper. Other lawyers sit bored waiting for their case to be called. In the public gallery are those also waiting for their case. Their eyes widen as I announce 'Final sentence two years and two months' and I see the alarm on their faces. Good God, am I going to get that for shoplifting?

The prisoner is led away yelling, 'Love ya, babe' — and he doesn't mean me.

Family call out, 'I'll bring your clothes. Stay staunch.'

They leave court, casting an evil eye at me as they go. I eye them back. I'm not going to retreat. If whānau had offered the right kind of practical support to that man, he might not have ended up here. Then, there's a tussle going on in my head. Maybe they tried hard, loved him, funded him, took away the car keys just as in the TV ad . . .

I do wonder. What careers are the children being encouraged to consider? Maybe farming or teaching in some families. In others, however, when the child is pushed through a small window as a precursor to a burglary or a mother takes the five-year-old on a shoplifting spree, I'm tempted to think career criminal is the only likely career ahead.

I remember the case of the woman, six months pregnant, in the supermarket with two children trailing behind her. She

managed to conceal a leg of lamb to round out the already
extended stomach. When she was stopped at the door and
questioned by security, the lamb fell to the floor. She jumped
back and yelled in an outraged voice, 'Where the fuck did
that come from?'

At the morning adjournment I leave too, wondering if I got
it right, if there could have been another way to reach that
young man, if prison will just be a breeding ground for his
resentment and anger.

Sentencing is a fine art and many in our community would
say we don't get it right. Longer sentences will deter them.
Make 'em pay. But it's more than picking a rabbit out of the
hat, or in this case a penalty. There are voices that must be
heard. Often, but not always, the police support a lighter
sentence or have no wish to comment. Probation often have
a view based on their previous experience of this defendant.
The victim's view must certainly be taken into account,
though their wish for revenge is not always in line with
appropriate sentencing guidelines. The offender's family's
plea for clemency along with the defendant's lawyer's
submissions all go into the mix.

It's interesting that those victims who initially want
the book thrown at a defendant for, say, a car stolen and
wrecked, or a punch thrown at a bar, sometimes have a
completely different view after attending a restorative
justice conference. There, they learn more than they knew
about this offender.

They also have the opportunity to spell out exactly what
the offence has cost them, not just in dollars. There is anger,
tears and ultimately a way forward, where the car thief or
young yobbo make good the loss in some way.

The whole encounter is attended by a coordinator, typed
up and provided to the judge in a report. It's not difficult to
read between the lines when the apology is shallow and the
reparation meaningless.

It seems to me everyone has a view on sentencing,

sometimes oblivious to the maximum prescribed by Parliament. I've read accounts complaining of six months' prison for domestic violence while elsewhere someone receives no prison time for causing a death. To conflate the two is to ignore the particularity of each offence, and they *are* unique, as is each offender. It's not a one size fits all. Nor will a 'job lot' approach work for drink drivers on any given day, for example.

On those days where a judge has 90 or more matters to hear, though, it must be tempting to herd all the shoplifters together and give them one speech about 'keep your hands off other people's stuff'.

There are days of sentencing in court when it's one after another: driving while disqualified, assault, sustained loss of traction by the boy racers, taking too many pāua from the ocean, dishonesty offences. The list rolls on in a seemingly endless fashion. Yet each defendant is entitled to be treated as if their case is the only one you are dealing with today.

Treat it all like a factory processing line and you've lost that innate knowledge of the essential dignity of each person before you. Sigh and look bored as if you'd rather be playing golf and, well, you should probably flag the job and get out on that golf course.

It's a strange position to be in as a judge passing sentence on someone. Not everyone agrees with you, least of all the defendant sometimes. In the end, though, you do what the job demands, and you have to ignore those voices that would belittle your efforts. There are plenty of them and some of them are strident.

I like the words of the US Supreme Court Judge Sonia Sotomayor, appointed in 2009, who has written some landmark rulings on civil liberties. She said once, 'I do know one thing about me: I don't measure myself by others' expectations or let others define my worth.'

I think to myself, that's a sentiment worth holding on to.

4 The custody tussle

NO NEW PARENT starts out with the thought: 'Now, how can I mess this up?' That small, helpless bundle invites love and commitment in most people. But the years roll on. Parenting is tough. So too are relationships. Add to that financial strain, sickness and the myriad things that can go wrong, and relationships founder on the rocks of good intentions.

And so they end up in court, arguing over everything from 'he gives them too much fast food' to 'she lets them stay up late'. The Family Court sees it all. At the heart of most disputes is an inability to work together as adults when the love has gone.

He doesn't provide clean clothes. She drops the children off late. He sends snaky texts. She put him down in front of the children.

Minor matters? Not worthy of court intervention? If the problem doesn't get aired and resolved, the losers are the children who will grow up with a tendency to depression, unable to form intimate relationships, vulnerable to drug and alcohol addiction.

No, not minor. It takes a big heart and a load of patience to be a Family Court judge, willing to wade in and see these 'minor' matters for what they really are: an enormous consequence for the next generation if the boil is not lanced now.

One of the most telling aspects of my work in the Family Court is the interview with children, often just before the court case begins. I conduct them in my chambers with the child and their lawyer present.

Time and time again, a child will tell me they want what is fair for both Mum and Dad. They want to do the right thing. They are sick of the arguing. If possible, they want their parents together again; if not, they want peace.

Sometimes they demonstrate a clear knowledge of the dispute, to such an extent that I know they have been shown affidavits written by their parents. Although they have been wrongly drawn into the custody tussle, they still retain some semblance of even-handedness.

I wish I could bottle some of the wisdom that emerges from children.

Their warring parents are hell-bent on proving a point, making the other pay. I occasionally remind them there was a time when they loved each other. Clearly hell will freeze over before *that* scenario is repeated.

They have hate down to a fine art.

They wouldn't call it hate.

After all, they have good reason to want to shut the other parent out of the children's lives. 'He's just a sperm donor.'

With attitudes like that, you'd think you were on a hiding to nothing to find any commonality or to effect a truce. Yet stranger things have happened.

The mediation process is presided over by a judge who meets with the opposing parties and their lawyers on the understanding that they, and not the judge, will decide matters. If they can't reach any agreement, it's off to court we go with the outcome determined by the judge, possibly an outcome that neither party would want. If a compromise is possible, so is a solution. I have always taken a fairly hands-on approach in such mediations, endeavouring to get the parties talking as much as possible but also offering my view on a best outcome, so they know what the judge thinks.

I've seen time and time again how two people walk into court, barely able to look at each other. An hour later after listening, really listening to the other, they can divest those old attitudes and soften their hearts. Now this is not all woo-woo stuff, but real gritty life-changing steps.

That's why I'm a fan of the judge-led mediated process. Rarely does a matter proceed to the next step. A mediation can be a reality check for those who think their way is right and the judge will see that. *Au contraire*, it's an opportunity to have those closely held beliefs aired. Usually they don't stand up to scrutiny.

The biblical story of King Solomon is about two mothers brought before him, each claiming the child belonged to them. Solomon's solution was to suggest cutting the child in half. The real mother couldn't imagine such a fate and, by her insistence that the child should live, even if she lost it, revealed herself as the true mother. People do reveal themselves, as the false mother did when she didn't contest the king's ruling.

These days, custody tussles are not only about mums and dads. Grandparents, aunts, uncles and state caregivers all vie for orders that will give them rights to the day-to-day care of a child. Sometimes, grandparents step in when their son or daughter is struggling with alcohol or drug issues. Here they are, in their sixties, thinking their child-rearing days are over and they are confronted with a completely foreign scenario, namely being parents again. I've seen the anguish on their faces, torn between love for their grandchildren and their reluctance to assume this burden.

What often makes it harder is the need to fight for their mokopuna in court, when a parent disputes that the care arrangements need to change. That can tear the adult relationships apart irrevocably.

While I might be tempted to think there are no winners

here, in fact there are. The children will be raised by people who love and cherish them, and that is all-important.

It's also not unusual now for the custody dispute to involve blended families.

In one rather complicated matter, the parties married, had two children and then separated. Then (or maybe before, who knows?) he had a relationship with her sister and, in what looked slightly tit for tat to me, she took up with his brother. Everyone had children, so sorting out contact arrangements was a bit complicated, made more problematic by the tension between all the adults. It's important for the judge to retain a neutral demeanour.

A face that says, 'You did what??!' might be okay over coffee or lunch, but not in the halls of justice where judges are expected to maintain a benign give-nothing-away look.

Children become the unwitting pawns in custody tussles. One of the saddest kinds of disputes involves the child becoming alienated from the other parent, and so they parrot the distasteful things about Mum or Dad to such an extent that the parent–child relationship can be irretrievably destroyed.

That occurred in a UK case, in which the judge apologised to the father who had spent eight years in an ultimately losing case. The judge made a scathing attack on the mother, pointing out the children would suffer long-term harm as a result of her bitter actions.[3]

It was Khaled Hosseini, an Afghani-US doctor turned writer, who said children aren't colouring books. You don't get to fill them in with your favourite colours. Moreover, children grow up and they don't always follow the party line. A child who realises in adulthood that they have been sold a line by the parent who raised them can feel very bitter at what they have lost.

A sad little girl once told me she didn't want to live with either parent and asked if she could stay with me instead. She wanted to bring her pet rat. I dearly wanted to gather

her up in my arms, take her home and show her a life free from conflict and discord. After all, it's the very least every child deserves. Someone once said that children are great imitators — so give them something great to imitate. Not tumult and turmoil.

I couldn't take her home. Not with a pet rat. I could tell jokes about them. What did one lab rat say to the other? I've got my scientist so well trained that every time I push the buzzer he brings me a snack.

Just don't ask me to raise one.

Pets can be a real challenge when they live only at one house, not to mention the transfer of loved toys, mementos and homework. But if parents can't sort their lives out over children, why are we surprised when leaders of countries can't do it either? It's really very basic and, at the same time, oh so complicated. Compromise. That means making concessions. For some, that's a bridge too far.

As the old joke goes, 'Why did the Republican get sunburn? Because the sunscreen instructed him to apply liberally and he wasn't willing to compromise.'

There have been endless revisions of the Family Court, resulting in fewer counselling services, less legal aid to sort out disputes and more hurdles to cross to get to a final hearing. All of these have been politically motivated, with little real consultation with judges and lawyers who do the work. Another review is currently under way. I do hope it will free up access to the Family Court and to specialist services that are vital for addressing conflict.

The Family Court was established in 1981. It deals with a wide range of legislation which goes well beyond custody issues. There are more than 20 separate pieces of legislation which govern matters in the court. They include challenges to a will, elder law, adoption, intellectual disability care, property disputes and mental health.

The court has operated in a less formal way, although since I became a judge, there has been a return to wearing gowns. If anything, greater formality is now encouraged. The Family Court Rules set out how a matter should be conducted, from the filing of documents to court procedure. There are 435 rules and navigating them is not easy.

Those who represent themselves in a custody matter are at a distinct disadvantage, not being conversant with the law. Even when they read up the law in advance, they are still giving weight to that old adage that a little learning is a dangerous thing.

There is a greater handicap, however. At the hearing, where a number of parties might be cross-examined, a self-represented litigant inevitably encounters problems. If they are questioning their ex-partner, it tends to deteriorate into a rant rather than properly put questions. There is a skill in cross-examination that takes a lawyer years of experience to develop and refine.

Time and again, I've had to pull back a questioner from either irrelevant or abusive lines of question.

'Your mother never liked me, did she?' 'Your second cousin is a paedophile, correct?' or questions that are actually statements: 'I'm going to bugger off to Aussie if I don't win this case and it will be all your fault.'

Not for nothing does a student spend four years doing a law degree. The risk of informality in a courtroom is that people think anything goes. They're wrong.

There used to be criticism that the Family Court was a secret court as it generally wasn't open to the media and decisions couldn't be released to the public. That clamour has died down as rules have relaxed, but I've rarely seen a representative of the media in any Family Court hearing.

Decisions are now anonymised and certain details changed to protect children, but a lot of Family Court decisions are available for perusal on the court's website, for those who can't sleep at night.

I've used the term 'custody' throughout this chapter, as the meaning is readily clear. But the Care of Children Act refers to 'day-to-day care', which I think is rather clumsy, although it does get away from the ownership idea of custody which has become a bit archaic.

I've often pondered what happens to those children whose parents spend years in court — and that does happen. In one memorable case, the parents were fighting from the time they separated when the child was three until he reached 11. Admittedly, the dispute was punctuated by some periods of truce, but they were fleeting.

At times, I've wondered whether the child would be better off in state care and went so far as to voice that in one matter. While that was enough to drag the parents back to reality in that case, the thought remains.

Let's raise children who won't have to recover from their childhood. Or as Frederick Douglass, the American escaped slave and statesman, put it: it is easier to build strong children than to repair broken men.

5 What's yours is mine

RELATIONSHIP PROPERTY DISPUTES would, on the face of it, seem more straightforward than arguments over children. After all, we're only talking about stuff. Right?

Take the much-loved dog, or that collection of Lladró, or the bach that one side of the family have visited annually for generations. As the law currently stands, couples who've been together for three years or more are covered by the equal sharing provisions of the Property (Relationships) Act 1976. Those treasures will have to be sold and the money divided, or they will be retained by one with a cash adjustment to the other.

I've seen property disputes played out in court over days or weeks with valuers and accountants for each party slogging it out; the fees involved are ultimately more than the value of the property in dispute. 'It's the principle of the thing' I've heard more times than I care to remember. But is it really that or more a question of revenge? And how far does revenge get you in the end?

One of the best books I have ever read addressed head-on the difficult matter of wanting revenge in circumstances where the author could be forgiven for holding on to hate. Edith Eger wrote *The Choice*, in which she described her journey from the Nazi death camps where she lost so many family members to America where she became a psychologist. She described attending a conference which turned out to be located in the place of Hitler's former home and realised revenge doesn't make you free. She forgave Hitler, because, as she put it: 'As long as I was holding on to that rage, I was in chains with him, locked in the damaging past, locked in my grief.'[4]

Aside from those parties who settle their property disputes in an honourable fashion (and they don't usually darken our doors), the Family Court is an arena in which not only revenge but all kinds of hurts are on display, sometimes wrapped up in jollity.

I recall a conference attended by Bob who's loud and abrasive and on to his third wife. His now ex-wife Mary is thin and fearful, though I detect a hint of steel. Bob wants to get on with the show. He thinks his humour will achieve that.

'Hey judge, did you know I stole my ex's wheelchair when we split. Guess who came crawling back?' Mary flinches but gives him an evil eye. I suppress a judicial snort. 'Behave, Bob.'

Some parties employ devious means to deal with property after separation. Chattels mysteriously disappear in the night, a car is sold to a mate for a dollar and, in the worst example, the family home is burned down. I've come across all those scenarios in court.

That's the kind of rancour I recall happening when I was a lawyer, when he got the wine collection but discovered to his horror she'd emptied every bottle first before the handover.

We've all heard of clothes being cut up, the new partner lambasted on Facebook or the car targeted. Cars are a favourite for revenge. Sugar in the petrol tank, tyres slashed, car keyed, and always, 'Well, it wasn't me. She can't prove it.'

Perhaps they're relying on the concept of beyond reasonable doubt, safe in the knowledge there are no witnesses. Aha! But the Family Court's standard of proof requirement is lower than that in the criminal jurisdiction. On the balance of probabilities is enough and so nasty texts and pejorative statements in his affidavit, coupled with his evasive answers on cross-examination, are enough to convince a judge.

You did it, you slimy toad. I omit the last phrase from my judgment.

People are hurt and feeling betrayed. I get that. I get too that some get stuck in their pain. The court often sees litigants when their grief is raw and new. If they can move past that, they have a better chance of settling a property dispute. It was Buddha who said, 'You can only lose what you cling to'. Letting go sounds easy. I know it's not, but it does make room for the life that is waiting for us.

For some, especially women, the end of a relationship spells real hardship. Even if they're left with half the assets, it's often not enough to buy a house.

Meantime, he's got his career and can recover financially in time. She's also got the kids, which impedes any prospect of a full-time job or retraining in that career she had 20 years ago, before the kids came along.

It was partly because of that scenario that the Property (Relationships) Act came into being, aimed at redressing the balance for women and including the provision (in section 15) for an extra lump sum, if being at home with children affected her income-earning ability.

Surprisingly, there have been relatively few applications of this kind and I wonder if this provision will survive future amendments to the act.

Relationships are a challenge at the best of times. When they end acrimoniously, the sky's the limit. I see you can get an app to catch a cheating spouse. At least we have moved past the days of needing to prove fault to obtain a divorce. Now, you can ask the Family Court to dissolve your marriage or civil union if you have been living apart for two years, at least one party is domiciled in New Zealand, and there's a view by one party that the marriage is over.

That doesn't stop some seeking a hearing to stop the divorce going ahead. Perhaps there are religious reasons or maybe the date of separation was a sham. It can be a bit more complicated when one lives overseas, decides to end the marriage, says nothing to the other, and then tries to get a divorce, claiming it was all over years ago.

In Australia the law requires only one year apart before a divorce is granted. In one case, my friend was the lawyer acting for a devout Catholic woman who was opposing the divorce on the basis that they had not been apart for a year. She had assiduously marked on the calendar the number of occasions they had had sex. She was questioned in some detail and, yes, could confirm that conjugal relations occurred at those various times.

Then the husband took the stand and he was cross-examined. The dates were put to him. He tried to object to the question, but the judge wasn't having any of it and insisted he must answer. Yes, he reluctantly conceded, those dates were correct, but 'they were just moments of weakness'.

To which the judge replied, 'I wouldn't call it that,' and declined to grant the divorce.

The other scenario that is often presented to the Family Court involves an application to declare the marriage void *ab initio*, from the beginning. The grounds for such an application might range from 'we were wed in a television show and never met before that', to 'we only married to benefit as uni students'.

While neither of those situations is likely to be successful, there is one area that the Family Court has seen with increasing frequency and that is marriages which have been arranged by relatives, usually involving a young woman, and usually with a degree of duress.

There is a cultural element that requires sensitivity. In more than one such case, I have granted the application, finding there was no real commitment to the marriage on the young woman's part. It was everyone else who made the commitment.

Such marriages bring risk, particularly when the parties are very young, so the law has been amended recently to cover 16 and 17-year-olds who wish to marry or enter into a civil union. They must have the approval of a Family Court judge under the Minors (Court Consent to Relationships) Legislation Act 2018.

This is not some sort of 'well, I like the cut of your jib', or 'you seem mature to me' kind of once over lightly by the judge. Nor is it an old-fashioned paternalistic interfering busybody intervention.

The increase of different ethnicities choosing to live in New Zealand brings a range of views about marriage and, with it, a need to protect young people against forced marriage.

It is significant then that the new law was passed by Parliament unanimously. That kind of cross-party support is rare and demonstrates the level of agreement about the issue.

When someone applies for such consent, the judge will appoint a lawyer for the applicant and may also ask for a cultural report to provide further information to the court.

In one such application that came before me, they were both 18, already had a child who was nearly two and she was expecting a second. I was able to use my best mother voice to quiz them about the responsibilities of marriage and parenthood. It was significant to me that both sides of the family were also in court. This very young couple had familial support, he had a job, and they both saw marriage as a serious commitment to which they wanted to pledge themselves. I granted the order.

Delays in the Family Court have meant that property matters are lower down the pecking order of priority than, say, child matters. So it's not unusual for a relationship property dispute to drag on for two, three or four years through court.

Those who eventually get to a hearing are bitter indeed. They wanted revenge and now here they are stuck in a courtroom watching their potential share of property disappear in legal fees. But forgiveness is off the cards.

As Anne Lamott, one of my favourite writers, once said, 'Not forgiving is like drinking rat poison and then waiting for the rat to die.'[5]

Or as Jodi Picoult put it, 'When you begin a journey of revenge, start by digging two graves: one for your enemy and one for yourself.'[6]

Given the equal-sharing provisions of the current legislation, you'd be forgiven for wondering why any disputes reach the court anyway. House, car, business, KiwiSaver, family chattels, all need to be valued and sold or a cash adjustment made if one party keeps some or everything. And the magic word is 'valued'.

Take a house, for instance. You can either get a real estate appraisal or, if you want to be more precise, a registered valuation, but then there's the matter of adjustments.

Say our ebullient Bob has stayed in the family home after separation and claims he's done work for which he wants to be reimbursed. Mary has moved on, in all ways, and doesn't want Bob or the house, but she does want him to pay occupation rent for the time he's lived there.

Then you have at least three legal issues: the correct value of the house, assessing the reimbursements to Bob, and calculating occupation rent.

Chattels can be tricky as they are generally used items and therefore assessed at their second-hand value; that is, what a dealer would give you. But Mary's unhappy because $50 is put on the value of the table and chairs, and it will cost her significantly more to buy a dining-room suite.

Perhaps one party claims a chattel has an inflated value, but when it's suggested that *they* keep it for that value, they're not interested. They only want the other to buy it at that price.

When couples argue in court over a list of chattels, which include such minor items as wooden spoons or a sandwich maker, you know you want to grab that wooden spoon and start handing out some primitive justice of your own. These thoughts you keep to yourself.

Sometimes, people take a while to come to the realisation that the house one of them bought 10 years ago before the marriage is now a 50:50 asset. 'But we were only together four years and she did nothing in the house' is a plaintive call I've heard. The fact she washed his shirts, cooked his meals and worked alongside him in the business is forgotten in a haze of recriminations. Even if she did do nothing, well, the exceptions to equal sharing are few, and the path to them is narrow.

I remember at the conclusion of one settlement in which a consensus had been reached, not quite a win–win as she had been recognised with a cash sum after a relatively short marriage while her overseas assets were protected, as being outside New Zealand's jurisdiction. He looked a bit down but relieved it was all over. In the chit-chat that followed, his lawyer told him I was retiring shortly. 'Lucky you,' he said morosely. 'I'll be working till I'm 95 paying her off.'

At that point, I keenly felt the favoured position I held, my retirement assured and relationship intact. Like the mental health patients, I knew it can all change in a heartbeat. I'm very grateful for what I have. As someone once said, gratitude turns what we have into enough.

What's the answer then when a relationship ends and there's stuff? Well, you could just see it as stuff and Marie Kondo will tell you what to do with *that*.

You could just walk away. After all, if the relationship was that toxic, you now have your freedom, and what price would you put on that?

Or you could opt to drag it out, fight and spit over every chattel, hide bank accounts, sink the boat, crash the car, then hope the judge is employing blind justice. Good luck with that.

6 The eye is on you

FROM THE FIRST TIME I climbed the stairs to the bench and looked out over clients and lawyers, I knew life was going to be different.

Until then, for 13 years I'd been facing the other way, always watching the judge closely, wary when they were grumpy, warier still when a judge would remove his glasses, wipe his eye and sigh heavily.

Now it was me. And just as I had watched the bench closely for any sign of wandering inattention, I knew that I would be under similar scrutiny. Was I going to be a crabby, roll-your-eyes, nod-off kind of judge when the going got tough? Or was I better than that?

You'll have to ask all those who appeared before me for that answer.

I did make a conscious decision though. From the start, I would be respectful to defendants and lawyers. I would eyeball people, not look around or beyond them. I would try not to humiliate or browbeat them. If I ever got in the chair grumpy or frazzled after a sleepless night or family drama, I would try to put that aside and concentrate on the task at hand.

Well, that was the plan. Events and people would conspire to test me to my limits at times.

'Fuck you judge' was the shout of a departing defendant,

angry that his bail had been revoked. 'No, fuck you' I always wanted to retort, but I held my tongue, thinking of the media presence, my children and the Chief Judge all at once.

Judges are meant to be dignified and moderate. If their behaviour is unseemly, an unhappy punter can lodge a complaint with the Judicial Conduct Commissioner. Occasionally someone may have a genuine grievance to air but, in the main, I suspect, not so much.

I was the subject of three complaints during my time on the bench. None were upheld. One remained with me as a reminder that we don't all share the same approach to the ins and outs of grammatical expression. In my decision I struggled to record the defendant's appalling spelling and grammar and the judgment was littered with '(sic)' to show I'd faithfully repeated the writer's words, even if they were misspelt.

For example, as I read in one affidavit, 'this is reely (sic) a waste of my time. The truble (sic) is Xyante shudn't (sic) live with her mother becus (sic) she won't help her to get a good edukashun (sic).

The complainant told the Judicial Commissioner that I had inserted 'sic' words and therefore changed the meaning. It was enough to make you sic.

When a person loses their cool in court, as often happens, there are ways a judge can respond. Ignore it, which at times is best as it takes the heat out of the situation. Puff out that chest and demand an immediate apology if you're feeling superior. Or make a joke of it if you're quick enough off the mark. Or send them to the cells to cool off. The trick is to be ready. A lawyer was cross-examining a father, who replied, 'I'm not answering until he wakes up.' The judge responded, 'I'm awake. I'm listening with my eyes closed.'

I was confronted one day with an outburst, not from the defendant to whom I'd declined bail but rather from his supporters at the back of the court.

As they attempted to leave, they made loud and colourful

observations about my heritage, complete with explicit hand gestures. Then they fled, which was to be expected.

I asked court security to bring all three women back into court and then asked lawyers present to talk with them about their behaviour and remind them that contempt of court is a charge which carries a maximum of three months' prison. Moreover, unlike other offences, the sentence imposed is what a person serves. No time off for good behaviour.

When they returned, the first was tearful and, through her lawyer, apologised profusely, saying the defendant was her brother and she 'just lost it'.

The second handed up a letter she had written. She was 16, the mother of a two-year-old. 'I'm better than this,' she wrote. 'I shouldn't have sworn at you. I know you're just doing your job, even if it is a stink one.'

I read into that an apology.

The third apologised through her lawyer but left me with the distinct impression she'd quite like to have another go at me, judging by her staunch and angry stance.

I talked to them about the court, how it is an institution that must be respected, because of what it stands for, and that offending the court is much worse than offending me personally.

The third young woman looked around at the walls, wondering to herself, I imagined, how on earth the walls could be offended.

I don't think she got it, but maybe her friends would explain it to her. They learned a lesson that day about respect for the judicial function, and that courtroom walls are really, really important. If that's all they got, it was better than nothing.

When the eye is on you, make sure you get it right. I remember one busy day in the criminal court. A young man was standing in the dock wearing a T-shirt that said, 'Quitting is for Quitters'. He was facing his seventh drink-driving charge and had pleaded guilty. I climbed into him about his alcohol consumption and his seemingly arrogant T-shirt. But, apparently, he had given up the drink and was proud of quitting. I got the message completely wrong. Humility (and an apology) was called for that day and, not for the first time, I felt like a total twit.

Occasionally a party in court will not shut up. No amount of shushing them, no tug on the sleeve from a nearby lawyer, nothing will do it. Once they start, they think they're on a roll.

If the offending words are a genuine grievance, I'm likely to let it go. If it's a rant pure and simple, I may elect to leave the court — it's hard to rave to an empty chair.

On one occasion, however, when I returned the defendant was still going, barely pausing for breath. I didn't know if he had mental health issues. I suspected not. Before I had a chance to launch into my contempt-of-court speech, he reached a crescendo, spat in my general direction and ran for his life out the door. Good move. I was tempted to send security after him but figured it would be a long time before he slowed down to take a breath. The security people are valuable. We need them in court, not racing through the city after posturing blowhards.

I suspect these little interludes are refreshing for lawyers who sit in the court all day, waiting their turn and wondering when the fun is going to begin. They know their submissions, worthy as they are, are not going to light a fire under any judge. It does make for a bit of variety when a prisoner lets rip from the dock or leaps over said dock, hell-bent on reaching the judge or police sergeant. The instructions to a judge from the security team are always to leave the court, as quickly and quietly as you can.

Often it's the judge who is the target of all that ire. Remove them and the heat dissipates quickly.

I recall one such occasion when the prisoner made a leap. He was cut short by the quickly extended leg of a lanky lawyer, who then followed that up with a tackle any All Black would be proud of.

Best submission by a lawyer, ever.

Throughout this little escapade, the judge must retain a sense of decorum. No high fives or fist victoriously punching the air, tempting as it might be.

A man in Russia was facing a charge of murdering his sister. He appeared in court, in a bulletproof enclosure which had four walls but no roof. He made a valiant and highly amusing attempt to escape through a ceiling panel, with three bailiffs climbing after him.

They grabbed his leg, only to end up holding an empty pant leg. More bailiffs arrived.

The escaping prisoner slowly disappeared, then reappeared. Finally, order was restored as he was brought back to the enclosure to get dressed.

Perhaps the prize for the most innovative New Zealand escape attempt goes to the gentleman who was assisted in his cunning plan by a friend who diverted the guard's attention by passing the prisoner a piece of chocolate. The guard was wondering whether the chocolate was worth confiscating or eating, and the prisoner ran.

One American judge did not get the memo about departing the courtroom if a furore erupted. When two defendants up on misdemeanour charges made a sudden and unexpected leap for freedom, the judge threw off his robe and ran after them. He followed them both down three flights of stairs and nabbed one. What a star! Maybe every new judge should have similar training for sprint and tackle, just in case.

I'm convinced American judges do it differently, not only in chasing a fleeing defendant. One judge, who had been convicted of unlawful interference in a public contract, was back in court after the appeal process had been exhausted. The presiding judge had the unenviable task of committing her to prison for six months, which was the sentence of the judge who originally heard the matter. Rather than simply accompanying the guard, the defendant had to be hauled out of court. Not a good look for any person but particularly unpleasant to see a judge dispatched in this way with her high heels dragging behind her.

I always said to myself that when my retirement date drew closer, perhaps even on the last day, I would take the opportunity to say all those things I had held back, I suppose in a kind of wilful payback. Childish I know.

All those politically inappropriate observations that would make headlines and draw ire. To the pregnant mother of 10: 'Isn't it time you got your tubes tied?'

To the errant well-to-do father always bad-mouthing his ex to the children and writing his affidavits in capitals: 'Stop shouting at me, you arrogant prick.'

Or to the rather pompous lawyer prefacing his submission to the court with a 'Has Your Honour ever considered. . .?': 'No, you great steaming git, I know what you're going to say, and if stupid could fly, you'd be a jet.'

When the eyes are on you, there is a certain expectation, and it's a reasonable one. You will be fair and measured. That will continue for the duration of your judicial life.

Shakespeare's Polonius offered advice to his son Laertes in *Hamlet* which rings true today for any judge, apart from the less than inclusive language:

'Give every man thy ear but few thy voice;
Take each man's censure, but reserve thy judgment.'

Wise words from the bard. Sometimes when the eye is on you, it is better to say less and endeavour to look wise.

Or, in the words of the oath that each judge takes at the start of their judicial career: I promise to do the job 'without fear or favour, affection or ill will'. It's simply put, and yet the wisdom of those words run deep. Honourable words that accompany you throughout your judicial career. They are a lot to live up to.

And so, I never felt able to speak as freely as I might have wished.

Couldn't write a letter of protest to the newspaper.

Couldn't give the finger to a lane-hopping driver.

Couldn't yell at the ref at a rugby game and tell him where to put his whistle.

And certainly couldn't say what I *really* thought. That is true for us all, though, from time to time. Even without the judicial imperative, it's better to bottle up those thoughts and say nothing — be thought of as an idiot, rather than speak and remove all doubt. Whether Abraham Lincoln or Mark Twain or my great-grandmother originally said it, it's good advice.

I knew as long as I was a judge and the eye was on me, no matter how much I disliked an individual, despised their politics or manner, fair treatment had to be the norm. And that's the way it should be for every judge. But why stop at judges? What if we all felt constrained by the need for measured behaviour when the eye was on us?

Now that would be something to see. I'm not talking about simply good behaviour but about being decent because we're human and that's what humans do. Couldn't we all agree on that? Or as my mother would say, 'Well, I'm unanimous on that.'

7 **How it began**

WHAT YOUNG GIRL goes through school dreaming of becoming a judge one day? Probably very few. A fair number may set their sights on being a lawyer, though no one ever said that to me at any of the four high schools I attended.

My dream was different. Before I started school, my mother read to me, a lot. Stories and poems that I learned by heart. One of my earliest memories was standing in front of my class in what was then known as primer one, reciting an A.A. Milne poem.

Never shy about coming forward, I was sent to speech lessons, entered competitions, and sat exams, eventually gaining my LTCL diploma. All of this was fodder for the dream of becoming an actor and working in theatre. My first role at the age of six was playing the little drummer boy in the Christmas play. I got to whack the drum with gusto, which seemed more satisfying than playing Mary, who just sat there.

On leaving school, I worked in radio. It was NZBC in those days, situated on The Terrace in Wellington. I was never a very good radio cadet. My heart was elsewhere, playing roles in amateur and then professional theatre at Downstage. Back in 1970, there were few opportunities for a budding thespian, though the occasional TV commercial came my way.

Then I had the opportunity to travel New Zealand with a drama quartet visiting schools and putting on two to three performances a day. That was too tempting to resist, so I said goodbye to my cadetship, and we went on the road.

Funny, you could tell what kind of audience the children would be by their principal. An engaged and enthusiastic school principal was replicated in the audience. The worst was one who, just five minutes into our performance, interrupted to ask if any students needed to put in their lunch orders. That call of 'sausages, filled rolls or drinks' kind of killed the mood of the play, not to mention the attention of actors and audience.

Then London was calling, or so I imagined. Time to do my OE, coupled with hopefully treading the boards. I started working two jobs to save the fare. In the evenings I worked as a waitress and developed the practice of using an accent, say Irish for one table, German for another and so on. This was 1972 and there weren't a lot of tourists about, otherwise I could have been busted by a real German speaker, but it was a great opportunity to use my acting skills on hapless diners.

I compared the cost of flying versus ocean liner. It was $380 to go the slow way. Six weeks on a boat. $420 to fly and I'd be there quicker.

I took off on 3 September 1972, complete with hot pants and a clumsy big bag containing my hair dryer with its long, snakelike tube. Drying your hair was a business in those days.

I managed to get an actor's equity card on the strength of work I'd done in New Zealand, but England was a different kettle of fish. It became apparent my Kiwi accent would do me no favours.

I spent hard-earned money on a voice teacher. Her claim to fame was that she'd helped Richard Chamberlain lose his twangy American accent for a role. She was very disapproving of my vowels and eventually they were chopped into little bits and replaced by more rounded sounds that were a source of amusement to my Kiwi mates. My 'it' had become 'eet' and 'New Zilan' now 'New Zeeelaaand'.

Back home, I'd rarely experienced being turned down for a role. Now, despite my freshly polished vowels, auditions resulted in disappointment, all the time. The dream was wavering and at some point I decided to travel, have fun and park the dream for some later date.

Not long after that, I met Mike. We returned to New Zealand, got married and had three children. And that took care of the next decade. All the while, the dream was simmering. Occasionally, I ran a drama group or recorded plays for Radio New Zealand.

When we had the chance to live in Switzerland for three years while Mike pursued theological studies, I discovered something I'd never taken to before. Swiss regulations meant I too had to study, and I launched into classes, research and writing papers, with a gusto that surprised me. I also wrote and presented a series of one-woman shows about women in history who remained invisible.

We returned home, me with a yearning to do something that was as yet undefined. With Mike's encouragement, I went to university, just to dip my toe into academic waters to see if I could.

My grades were mostly As and one day as I read another letter from the head of department encouraging me to do my degree in their department, my ever-supportive husband said those now magic words, 'Why don't you do a law degree?' I'd never contemplated being a lawyer. After all, it was a long way from the theatre. Wasn't it?

But here was an opportunity that seemed right. All three children were at primary school. Money was tight, but in 1987 student fees were a thing of the future and the Family Benefit scheme paid me a modest amount each week. I decided to go for it.

I set myself the challenge that I would have to get into law school on the same criteria as school leavers, not the slightly easier level for adult students. Subsequently, my average of A– over six subjects was enough to achieve that, and there was much celebration among the family that Mum was going to school too and would one day be a real lawyer.

For my part, it was an opportunity to give voice to those ideas I held about justice and fairness. I'd seen first-hand how our psychiatric community was relegated to second-class citizens and my feminist heart had awakened in Switzerland with the study and books I'd read. Now I wanted a room of my own as well.

My newfound independence came in the form of a bright red 50 cc motor scooter, called a Nifty Fifty. It was a quick journey to uni and the petrol bill was $2 per week. My friends were disapproving of this mode of transport, saying it was a death trap and I'd be knocked off by a car door. In the event, it wasn't that. It was a pedestrian running across the road against the lights, with whom I collided. I was knocked out and when I came to a gentleman was helping me up and offering me his card. Turns out he was in life insurance.

If the family were chuffed at my progression from mother to student, the church community were even more so. Each year, one of the elderly members of the congregation would give me money for books. She had been a young woman in the 1920s who went to art school hoping to make it her life's career. Marriage and children had put paid to that. She saw my efforts as doing what had been denied her all those years before.

When my energy flagged and I thought the study would never end, I said to a friend one day, 'I'll be 40 soon.' She replied with a common-sense wisdom, 'Well, you'll be 40 whether you finish the degree or not.'

I did play with the idea of going part-time, but the degree was four years on a full-time basis, and I hated the thought of being a perennial student who never left the place. I was desperate to get this degree under my belt and start practising real law. So I soldiered on.

I picked up radio work at ZB and Radio Pacific doing radio commercials and occasionally voice-overs for television commercials. The extra money was crucial to supplement our one-income family.

In the school holidays, Mike took the children away or they went to my parents, so I could have uninterrupted study time. That was a gift that I eagerly looked forward to.

Mature students often sit up the front in lectures because they are keen. In my case, I couldn't hear further back, but I was certainly keen.

I remember an early Torts class in which lecturer Bill Hodge was discussing the meaning of a tort, a civil wrong, and contrasting that with a criminal offence.

'What would you do if someone stole your car?'

A student responded, telling the story of how he'd discovered his daughter's stolen bike poking out of a neighbour's shed. 'And what did you do?' pondered the professor.

'I took my bolt cutters and went round there and got it back.' Grass-roots justice. The class let out a 'whew', whether of admiration or disapproval I'm not sure.

I enjoyed the lectures and research. With three other mature students, we formed a study group which proved to be enormously helpful. I was never a top student. My As dropped to Bs and I often worried that I wouldn't get a job after graduation. But at the end of the first year, I applied to and was accepted by all three of the big law firms for a summer job. While that was fun, I knew the big-firm mindset wasn't my cup of tea.

Most of the students were school leavers and, in my eyes anyway, seemed very confident about their future. I walked into the shared lounge one day to hear two male law students discussing their plans. They both wanted to become judges but agreed they wouldn't bother with the District Court — nothing less than the High Court for them. I've often wondered whether their supreme self-assurance was rewarded. For my part, I wouldn't even have *thought* such a thought, never mind voiced it.

When the day came and I completed my final exam, in Evidence, I arrived home to find the children had made and hung up a huge colourful banner in the lounge. 'Well done Mum' it read.

It was their accomplishment too.

My degree was awarded in 1992 from Auckland University.

The children were at the front of the queue waiting to get into the Auckland Town Hall where the graduation ceremony was held. Our son Matthew swooped in and sprawled himself along a row of seats. When it came time for me to receive my degree, I turned and bowed not to the assorted academics, but to the row of husband, three children and my parents. Their unwavering support had made this possible.

That led to a job in which the irony of 'acting for people' was not lost on me. I enjoyed court work and seeing clients, helping them find solutions. Back then, lawyers still wore wigs in the High Court and while I enjoyed the civil work there, the horsehair definitely put me off.

There I was. A lawyer, then an associate in a firm, and finally in 1999, the longed-for entry to partnership. That might have been the progression for me, but women then as now still struggle to make partnership.

The statistics issued by the New Zealand Law Society show what they describe as a glacial rate of improvement for women being admitted to partnership over the years. For example, it was 19 per cent in 2012 and 32.7 per cent in 2018. All that time, women have made up the majority of both law students and those practising law in New Zealand, yet when it comes to partnership and women on the bench, we are not equally represented.

I wouldn't say partnership was a barrel of laughs, and I could envisage the day when I went out as a barrister practising on my own. Before that occurred, I received a phone call from the then chief judge encouraging me to put my name forward for consideration as a judge. What, me, a judge? My fraud complex kicked in hard, reminding me of all the reasons why I wouldn't, shouldn't, couldn't even consider it. As always, Mike was my supporter and cheerleader.

It's hard going through the interview process, telling no one, waiting for months for the outcome, trying to concentrate on work, but knowing that my heart wasn't in it. Three months after the interview, I took the call at court, ironically underneath the sign 'No telephones'.

'You've got the job. But we need you to keep it confidential until the Governor-General signs your warrant.' This was just before Christmas and the GG signed the all-important document at the end of January 2006, leaving me two days to tell everyone and for the Dunedin court to arrange a swearing-in ceremony.

No mean feat, but they managed, complete with a piper and bagpipes.

At the ceremony, I referred in my acceptance speech to the words of Micah from the Old Testament. I said they would guide me in my job. The question is asked in the Book of Micah: what does the Lord require of you? The answer: to act justly, to love mercy and to walk humbly with your God. Good advice for anyone, but especially relevant for the role I was about to take on.

Once I became a judge, one of the first things I did was to go to a car dealer's with Mike. We were looking for a new car.

I spied a red Mercedes. It was a convertible with an automatic soft top, and leather upholstery.

This was so far from any car either of us had ever owned. Our first car was a 1949 Ford Anglia. Since then we'd had vans, an Austin Maxi and even, at one time, a Lada, fresh off the factory floor in Moscow. You get the picture.

We went home to have a final think about it. The next day, I woke up, no, I mean I *woke up*. Me in a Mercedes? It must have been a rush to the head.

A car had always represented a means to get from A to B,

though in the case of the Austin Maxi, that was debatable. I realised life may have changed, but not that much.

For me, the job was the culmination of a lot of things. That young girl who enjoyed speaking in front of crowds, who could make her voice heard and who felt passionately about a lot of things, who thought the theatre was her *raison d'être*, soon discovered the courtroom was where she belonged.

Listening to arguments, weighing up evidence, trying to find a fair outcome and, it has to be acknowledged, being bowed to on a regular basis was, I learned, all part of the job I loved.

Not once in 14 years did I yearn to try something else or want to give it all away. And so, when it did end rather abruptly, it was hard. I had yet to read John Lennon's words, 'Everything will be okay in the end. If it's not okay, it's not the end.'

8 The media: social and antisocial

MY DAD WAS A JOURNALIST, and I well remember cycling on my way to school and detouring to the *Marlborough Express* newspaper to deliver his copy. One day, when I should have been at school, he took me to court with him. In the tiny Kaikōura courtroom, it wasn't the judge I remembered or even the defendants, but Dad sitting at the press bench, scribbling away in his highly illegible script to keep up with all that was happening.

Dad went on to work for the New Zealand Press Association, then the DSIR in Palmerston North. He was always a wordsmith and I remember the day one of his articles was published in the *New Zealand Weekly News*. We were in the library at the time and he must have been chuffed because he handed me half a crown.

Dad was a great advocate of the book *The Elements of Style*,[7] perhaps more widely known as Strunk and White, and he often quoted it to me. For all its emphasis on reducing the rules of grammar and punctuation to produce greater brevity, the book nevertheless recognised the most important thing: writing is an act of faith not a trick of grammar.

Although I never aspired to journalism, I have retained

a healthy respect for those who go digging for the truth —
there are fewer of them now in the days of social media, but
they're still around. I know the importance of deadlines and
checking the facts and getting the story out there. So how
many journalists does it take to change a lightbulb? They'd
say, 'We just report the facts, we don't change them.'

As a newbie judge, I was about to be initiated into the
world of the media. I remembered that maxim: 'You have the
right to remain silent. Anything you say will be misquoted
and used against you.' I hoped not.

My baptism of fire came only months into the job. A
young boy had effectively been kidnapped by his grandfather
and spirited away somewhere. For five months, no one could
find him. Then, one day, his grandfather handed him in to
the police.

I had been doing mental health hearings that morning
and, on my return to court, there was an application for an
urgent hearing and 22 requests from various branches of the
media, wanting to attend court.

At that time, the Family Court was generally closed to the
media, although permission could be granted on a case-
by-case basis. I let them all in, figuring this was a matter of
national interest, though I didn't realise I would be delivering
a decision that would be reported word for word on the front
page of the *New Zealand Herald* the next day.

The difference between an oral and a reserved decision
is that the former is spoken at the conclusion of the hearing,
warts and all, while in the case of the latter there's time to
construct a rather more elegant tome.

By and large, I have been dealt with fairly by the media,
though on the occasion I discharged a hunter without
conviction because of his circumstances, I thought the
focus of reporting was more heavily weighted in favour of
the animal he killed, rather than the background which led
to the killing. If that sounds more like a lawyer talking, than
an animal rights advocate, it's good to remember there is

no place on the bench for being a proponent of any kind. We have to leave our pet causes at home, and our pets.

In another case involving animal cruelty, the front row of the public gallery was taken up by animal rights supporters wearing T-shirts announcing who they were. On that occasion, I was sentencing a man who had killed a puppy with a golf club, and the media sought to take a photo of the defendant. Defence counsel opposed that, on grounds I thought sounded reasonable. He said his client had children who were attending the local school and they had been subject to bullying because word had got round about what their dad had done.

In reply, the police argued, if that was the main basis for declining to identify the defendant, then the horse had already bolted, to mix the animals.

Ultimately, I allowed a photo to be taken of the defendant in the dock, which happened quickly, because the media remembered the last time he was in court, when permission was given and he quickly pulled down his hoodie over his face. Not so fast this time.

I did wonder on that occasion whether I should recuse myself as having a conflict of interest, because I owned a dog at the time. I was careful about conflicts, but this time thought, well, most people like dogs, and even if they don't, no one is going to be in favour of despatching an animal in such a brutal fashion. I had seen the photos which showed in graphic detail what he had done. I gave the defendant what was one of the highest prison sentences at the time for animal cruelty — two years and three months.

You hear the case, deliver your decision and that's it. No chance to tell the media why you saw the facts in a particular light and certainly no option of disclosing some hitherto confidential matters that even the police deem worthy of repression.

Once a decision has gone out into the world, it's at the mercy of the media and talkback radio and, of course, the

Appeal courts who, if called upon, must determine whether the application of facts and law was erroneous in any way.

I was incensed one day while wandering the streets at lunchtime to see a billboard outside a dairy proclaiming 'Judge gives bail to rapist'. That judge was me and it involved a *suspected* rapist. There's a big difference. I was so angry I wanted to throw the metal billboard through the dairy window. I didn't. My vivid imagination conjured up the next day's headlines, 'Judge denies bail to judge on the rampage'.

One of my colleagues heard a case where a man was charged with discharging a gun at a large vat of milk. He had an ongoing feud with his neighbour. All the milk drained out and the complainant wanted reparation of $4000. The judge wanted to say, well, there's no use crying over spilt milk, but saw the journalist in the press box, with pen poised. So she restrained herself.

Not so the lawyer who made a play on words about spilt milk and made it big in the paper the next day.

For a number of years, I had the opportunity to speak to journalism students. They were fresh-faced and looked, to me anyway, far too young to be embarking on such a demanding career. I tried to encourage them to stick to journalistic ethics: avoid sensationalism, be fair and impartial, and remember their first obligation is to the truth. We in New Zealand might think we are removed from the excess of such bastions as Fox News and their ilk. But our world has shrunk and now it's not just *Stuff* or our local newspaper to which we have access.

Social media has opened up new realms, with consequences. Or, as some say, social media is like waking up in a psychiatric hospital. You have no idea you're committed until you try to leave.

Everyone wants to share the minutiae of their day. Oversharing is the new tittle-tattle. Like the post: 'I once crashed my bike, skinned my elbow and hurt my knee. I'm telling you this now because we didn't have social media back then.' In fact, as the old joke goes, 'I've always wondered how my parents passed the time in the 70s and 80s without social media. I asked my 32 siblings and they've got no idea either.'

Undoubtedly social media can fulfil some useful function, but as someone who has never had a Facebook page, my observations of those who do is in line with the words of T.S. Eliot: 'distracted from distraction by distraction'.[8]

The proliferation of apps and social media sites might be designed to improve our lives, but occasionally they're just irritating as Dan Howell, a YouTuber and author, reported:

'I once got a notification from the BBC news app saying that a character in a show I was watching had just died! I thought that news notifications are supposed to be for impending natural disasters, not for just ruining my bloody afternoon.'[9]

Despite having a brother and sister-in-law who work in television, we don't have a TV and haven't for years. In fact, while our children were growing up, there was no telly in the house, our reasoning being they might learn more without it. I'm fortified in that view by Groucho Marx who once said, 'I find television very educational. Every time someone switches it on, I go into another room and read a good book.'

From time to time, my face did appear on TV in relation to a case. Some of my colleagues worked hard to ensure there was never a photo of them available to the media, and if they ever allowed cameras in the courtroom, it was to focus solely on the defendant, not the judge.

Maybe there's some wisdom in that, especially if you want to avoid being recognised in the supermarket and hectored by a member of the public. For my part, I figure if we are prepared to sit up there on the bench and make pronouncements on people's lives, then we should also be willing to be identified. That view of course is a double-edged sword, particularly when it comes to the more extreme members of our community.

Groups with an axe to grind can gain traction to a degree far in excess of their importance, if the media is having a quiet day.

Some fathers' groups, or mothers' groups for that matter, raise genuine issues via the media and keep us all on our toes.

Others seem hell-bent on a campaign of harassment which goes beyond court to a judge's personal life, impacting on their children and, at times, their personal safety.

When I was targeted by such a group, there was the risk they might interrupt our open day when we were selling our house. Mike threatened to join them bearing a placard reading 'Join us! The world needs more idiots'. Fortunately, it never came to that.

There was a Canadian case of a father in court for failing to pay child support. At the end of the hearing, the father made his way to the front of the court and attempted to place the judge under a citizen's arrest for 'crimes against humanity'. His attempt failed.[10]

There's certainly a place for protest as the 1981 Springbok tour of New Zealand demonstrated and many protests since — #MeToo and the recent Black Lives Matter anti-racist movement as I write. The media's obligation is to faithfully and objectively report such protest. On the other hand, giving a voice to bias and prejudice helps no one, least of all those who complain. Some websites really go to town, though what they hope to achieve I am not sure; for example:

'We say to our family court judges: smarten up your act, we're watching everything you do and fathers are talking to each other right around the country. Your reign of terror is coming to an end.'

That little piece of penetrating sagacity came from a fathers' website.[11]

Other sites tend to be merely a rant, and I guess we all need to let rip at times. But where the tone descends into inciting violence or making clearly defamatory statements, they go too far. One clearly fanatical website, reporting on a judge who had sentenced a man on a domestic violence charge, described the judge as 'evil' and said, 'May she be the victim of extreme male violence herself.' It is hard to find any redeeming quality in that piece of venom.[12]

In my first year on the bench, picketing at judges' homes led to the Principal Family Court Judge describing the protests as intimidatory and clearly intended to bring unacceptable pressure on the court.

There's a fine line between legitimate protest and a vendetta. The job of the Fourth Estate is to identify which is which.

It was the Victorian writer Thomas Carlyle who called the press 'the fourth estate of the Realm', seeing it as holding a watchdog role in our society. We can go back even further to Edmund Burke who repeatedly said, 'There were three estates . . . but in the Reporter's Gallery yonder there sat a fourth estate important far more than they all.'[13]

The press should serve as the voice of the people, speaking truth to power. That's not too much to ask, is it?

9 The dark side

NEW ZEALAND, along with the rest of the world, has recently lived through Covid-19. It started as a sudden rise in cases — an epidemic — in Wuhan, China. Spreading worldwide, it thus became a pandemic. It called for desperate measures to counter the infection rate that threatened to rise alarmingly. Fortunately, drastic steps were taken in New Zealand, and we are now hoping the virus may never take hold seriously in this country.

But there is another epidemic, and it's not an overstatement or exaggeration to describe it in those terms. Domestic violence afflicts our country, with an incident investigated by police every four minutes.

We think of the economic cost of Covid-19. Well, family violence costs our country between $4.1 and $7 billion each year. New Zealand has the highest rate of domestic violence in the developed world.[14]

If you want more statistics on all of this, in the year ended 31 March 2019, there were 1.32 million domestic abuse-related incidents and crimes reported to police. Of those, 746,219 were deemed by police to be related to domestic abuse.[15]

Put simply, family violence is our national shame.

How did we get to this state? Many wring their hands,

helpless. Others play the blame game. Let's look at an example taken from real life. A young Māori woman grows up in a home where Mum regularly got the bash. Her brothers responded to that by being handy with their fists at school. She, let's call her Aroha, turns her pain inward, afraid Mum somehow deserved it. She left home as soon as she could, doing a course at polytech, determined to succeed.

A young student there was kind to her. That felt strange and soon they were in a relationship. But he wanted her all to himself, checked her phone constantly and berated her if she went anywhere without him. She told herself it was because he really loved her.

She felt caught between the love she felt and the way her independence seemed to slip away. During an argument one night, he hit her, apologised profusely the next day and so a pattern developed.

Beatings followed by flowers.

They had two children. She knew if she left, she had no one to turn to. Besides, he'd find her and that would be worse.

Then her son started getting aggro at kindy, lashing out at other kids. She never made the connection with her brothers' behaviour, but a chance conversation one day was the turning point.

A lady at the bus stop helped her with the pushchair and they walked home together. Aroha unloaded her fears about her son. The older woman was perceptive enough to sense how abusive the adult relationship had become. She gave Aroha advice and a way out.

She suggested a lawyer, so she could get protection from the violence, and emergency accommodation thanks to Women's Refuge. Most importantly, she provided Aroha with a listening, non-judgmental ear.

Today Aroha is a trained social worker. She understands the dynamics of family violence and tells her story as a salutary tale to others. She is committed to working with Māori to break the intergenerational scourge of domestic violence. She understands the trap women fall into but is also wise to the futility of recrimination. 'Blaming solves nothing. We need big hearts to help both men and women choose a different path.'

I won't attempt to list the multitude of factors that contribute to family violence. Yes, it's power and control by men and, yes, colonisation has played a part. But there is much, much more. I think it's too easy for those unaffected by such violence to cast it aside as a poor people's problem or turn their back on what goes on next door.

My years in both the Family Court and the criminal jurisdiction taught me it happens across all ethnicities, to the privileged and the underprivileged, to men and to women.

I don't believe prison is the answer.

I agree with the words of the chair of a report, *Men Who Use Violence*, produced by the Family Violence Death Review Committee, released in April 2020.

Professor Jane Koziol-McLain said, 'To realise safety for women and children, we need to expand our gaze to better understand and interrupt the pathways men are on that lead them to perpetrate violence and harm.'

In an interview on that report in the *New Zealand Herald* on 30 April 2020, she said, 'Demonising men who use violence and solely relying on criminal sanctions and short-term interventions hasn't worked.'

As a judge, my options are limited. Stopping Violence programmes aren't always tailored to an individual's situation. A prison term might remove the offender from the home, but it often also takes the breadwinner or the one who cared for the children while the woman is at work. Sentences of intensive supervision at least allow for an offender to undergo remedial programmes and when that's added to judicial monitoring, it means a report is provided to the judge on the offender's progress every few months. Any backsliding or lack of commitment to rehabilitation can result in the offender being recalled to court for the judge to look at an alternative sentence, such as prison.

One of the sad aspects of family violence is that the victim is often reluctant to follow through with any prosecution. One of the most graphic examples I encountered was a case where he had stomped on her neck and the police photos showed the clear outline of a boot imprint.

When the matter progressed to a trial, she was reluctant, claiming it hadn't been like that. Maybe she was afraid of recrimination after the court case. Perhaps, put baldly, she loved him and wanted him back in the house. Or she believed it wouldn't happen again.

I don't know, but I have enormous sympathy for victims who think, 'This relationship, dysfunctional as it is, is as good as it'll ever get for me, so I probably should stick with him or I'll be alone.'

That is a common pattern for family abuse cases. Initially the woman contacts the police to report abuse of some kind. They visit the home and, with her permission, take photos and then a statement. At any point after the man is charged, she recants with a letter to the court, or an affidavit (which is a sworn statement, so lying invites a perjury charge), or in person.

She might perhaps leave it until the actual day of the trial and either doesn't turn up, whereby police have to locate and arrest her, or comes to court and, under oath, says she made it up.

When there is graphic evidence of physical abuse, denial is more difficult. Some say, 'Well, I hit him too.' But since he has never claimed to the police that he acted in self-defence, that argument isn't going to fly.

The law is changing. The court can rely on a prior consistent statement, regardless of whether the victim later recants.

I always felt uncomfortable putting the victim in the position of potentially breaking the law, either by not turning up to court or, worse, lying. It's bad enough being a victim of family violence, but the woman then tries to 'save' her man, the aggressor. If she's successful, it usually results in things being fine for a while. Then the whole cycle of abuse starts again.

There are indications of response to this epidemic at government level, with money being poured into various initiatives and recent legislation offering a modicum of protection for victims of family abuse.

The Domestic Violence — Victims' Protection Act 2018 gives employees who are victims of family violence the right to 10 days' domestic violence leave, access to short-term flexible work arrangements and the right to not be treated adversely in the workplace.

New Zealand is one of the first countries in the world to implement such a law.

It's a start.

If a victim can keep her job through an episode of domestic violence when, as studies show, the perpetrator has been known to hassle her at work or try to get her fired, she retains her all-important financial security.

Other laws have been amended to reinforce the need for safety for victims. The Family Violence Act 2018 took effect on 1 July 2019. It replaced the Domestic Violence Act passed back in 1995.

I remember a Family Court judge travelling the country in 1995 doing seminars on the then new legislation which incorporated a novel creature, called a Protection Order. He was explaining how such an order can be made in favour of a victim, who can, if she chooses, allow the violent person back into the home and later withdraw that permission if things get heated again.

He drew an analogy. 'It's a bit like those jackets that can be unzipped at the sleeve or shoulder. They're still a jacket but with different functions.'

After the seminar, a young lawyer came up to the judge and asked him where she could get one of those jackets; it was a case of listening but not really hearing.

The Care of Children Act has also been amended recently to add new provisions such as enabling the judge to make a Temporary Protection Order where there are concerns about an adult or child.

In the health sector, there are family violence intervention coordinators in all district health boards. Practical tools have been developed to enable health professionals to make safe interventions where they consider it necessary. First responders and nursing staff are less likely to accept at face value the explanation 'I walked into a door'.

Attempting to strangle someone is so dangerous and can lead to death within a couple of minutes, so the law has recently made it a separate offence. That law change came into effect in December 2018. Nine months later 1246 charges of strangulation had been laid; 97 per cent of those charged were men.[16]

Law change takes us so far. Attitudes must change too.

At grass-roots level, a revolution is needed. The 'It's Not OK' anti-violence campaign has done a good job of raising the profile about violence, and I always find it heartening to visit a small town which has a large banner on the outskirts proclaiming something like, 'Domestic Violence. It's Not OK Here'. Our prime minister's home town of Morrinsville is a case in point.

But more is required. If the national psyche were such that a slap, punch or verbal intimidation was outside the bounds of a decent society, how different we would be.

And lest there are any readers who think women are as violent as men, let me remind you of the findings of a study over the years 2009 to 2015. That found intimate partner violence was responsible for half of the 194 family violence deaths. In 98 per cent of the death events, women were the primary victims abused by their male partner.[17]

Sure, I've had cases of violence by women against men, harder to prosecute because men feel the helplessness and shame of not being able to deal with it. But the overwhelming tide of abuse runs the other way.

Owning up to being part of a society that allows family violence would prevent us from seeing it as someone else's problem.

It's *our* problem and the huge financial and emotional cost is a burden we all bear. We're all in it together, just as we have been fighting the enemy that is Covid-19.

The question is whether we have the same commitment to eliminate this scourge.

Too many people, adults and children, live in fear.

Family violence extends beyond hitting, kicking and punching. It includes the psychological aspects of violence — belittling and manipulative behaviour, abusing family pets in front of other family members, controlling and abusive actions such as isolating a person from family and friends, threatening suicide and other emotional manipulation.

Perhaps there is a carry-over from more historical times when women were treated as being 'owned' by their husbands. Maybe there are different cultural views about physical punishment and retribution. Or is it just that 'getting the bash' is still regarded in some circles as acceptable behaviour?

To all of that, I say not good enough.

Changing attitudes about family violence will only happen when we work together for change. Like Aroha from our story, change occurs from something as small as a conversation, or a reaching out, but then all revolutions start small. Mother Teresa said, 'I alone cannot change the world, but I can cast a stone across the waters to create many ripples.'

10 The unexpected

C.S. LEWIS SAID IT WELL: 'The great thing, if one can, is to stop regarding all the unpleasant things as interruptions of one's "own" or "real" life. The truth is of course that what one calls the interruptions are precisely one's real life.'

In the life of a judge, the unexpected always happens. The prisoner who jumps the dock. The lawyer who falls asleep (though both events not usually at the same time). The witness whose testimony makes a surprising U-turn. They all remind us that this is part and parcel of real life, not an adjunct or minor interruption to it.

A colleague of mine was in court and the defendant was looking extremely agitated, as if he might leap from the dock to the bench. Two security guards sensed this and both moved quickly to surround him. The defendant, realising what they were doing, was stunned. 'Oh my God Your Honour, I'm not coming for you. You're bootiful.'

One gentleman, whom we'll call Bernie Blot, informed me from the dock one day that he wouldn't answer to the name on the charging document. He preferred to be known as Lord Hawthorne Quincy. I had to be sure we had the right defendant and finally inveigled out of him that, yes, the birth date I read out was his. There were no apparent mental health issues and he had not taken any steps to change his name, as far as the police or I knew. It was a busy court day with lots of people waiting for their matter to be heard.

I detected a certain smugness on his face as if to say, 'Gotcha, judge. You can't do anything with me when I don't answer to my name.'

I assumed my most thoughtful look. Then 'Thank you Lord-Hawthorne-Quincy-Bernie-Blot. Adjourned to the next callover. Stand down.' He was a bit miffed, though not too much. After all, I'd given voice to his loftier moniker.

There are those, especially in the Family Court, who choose to represent themselves. Some genuinely cannot afford a lawyer. Others think they can do a better job. They are usually mistaken and, curiously, most often men.

They are invariably not familiar with court etiquette or the Family Court Rules which govern proceedings. They bow very low (from the waist) which is not necessary from a layperson and not that low from anyone.

They often don't realise that a judicial conference is simply to determine the next step in the proceedings, such as how many witnesses are required, whether more affidavits should be filed, how long should be allocated for the fixture, and so on.

They want to tell the story, the whole story of the dispute, how it should be resolved, and they don't take kindly to being interrupted. They also get a reputation among the Family Court staff as being difficult. If they are loud and truculent towards me, it's likely to be much worse for staff, who get a double dose because they don't wear a black gown and can be dismissed as 'staff'.

When I get one of these unexpected tirades, I find the best way forward is to listen for a while until they have to take a breath and then raise my right hand, palm facing out. Most reasonable people see that as a stop. If that fails, it's both hands with the eyes momentarily closed. The fallback is the stern mother voice, all the while, I'm thinking, remember when I asked for your opinion? Yeah, me neither.

The self-represented person has learned from (some) lawyers that 10 words are better than one and big ones better than small. They describe themselves in overinflated terms. Occupation: advocate-general, which sounds to me like a job far more important than our Attorney-General or Governor-General. They are verbose and garrulous. They blather on, sometimes amusing the bench with malaprops. Like the memorable client buying a farm and complaining to his solicitor that the sheep were awfully thin. 'They're emancipated!' he declared.

Sheep free from the rigours of farm life! Free at last!

On a more serious note, an Australian study, published in 2020 by the *Melbourne University Law Review*, made an interesting discovery. It was written by law graduate Amelia Loughland, who found that an analysis of interruptions, drawn from transcripts over a two-year period in the High Court there, showed that women judges were much more likely to be interrupted than their male counterparts. Lawyers talking over them were the chief culprits and, curiously, that pattern increased when a woman took over the reins as Chief Justice in 2017.

The study looked at possible explanations for these male interrupters. Were the judges speaking more than their male counterparts? No, not that. Other possibilities were considered and rejected. The research deduced that institutionalised gender bias was at play. Even when a lawyer realised they had interrupted the judge, they were far more likely to be deferential and apologetic to the male judge than to a female one, as revealed in the transcript.

The writer concluded she wouldn't want to suggest that those men disrespected the females, but rather that it was completely unconscious behaviour. Hmm.

Ms Loughland also, somewhat depressingly, noted that her research 'should draw attention to the fact that despite women's formal equality, they still face barriers in being treated as equal to their male colleagues, even at the pinnacle of their legal careers'. Depressing indeed.

It may be apparent that I often use humour as a weapon with which to bash others over the head, metaphorically of course. Sometimes I wish I was an octopus so I could slap eight people at once.

When the unexpected happens, humour is a lifesaver, in the face of chauvinism, bias and all the other isms.

There's no doubt humour can be a great backstop — even in your head. Law is a serious business and you are expected to deal with those unexpected events with decorum. Which is a shame really because occasionally I want to break out, tell a joke, lighten the mood.

Speaking of the unexpected, sometimes someone comes into your life out of nowhere, makes your heart race and changes your life forever. We call these people cops.

But back to the task at hand. The unexpected can confer a certain *joie de vivre* that lightens the humdrum of life.

An older, well-dressed man bounced into court one day, made a lot of noise getting himself comfortable in the public gallery and then, when his name was called, leapt to his feet and proceeded, with a flourish, to offer me an exaggerated bow complete with swishing hand movements. He was then invited by court security to proceed to the dock, which he did, again with an almighty flourish.

I was starting to think I was back in the theatre.

The charge was read out. I asked him if he understood.

'Madam, I do,' he said in a voice that sounded like Sir Ian McKellen.

I then asked if he had a lawyer. 'Pray no,' came the reply. Was he sending me up? I struggled on. I established that he wanted to be sentenced today without the benefit of a lawyer. It was a minor charge of disorderly behaviour. I couldn't imagine this distinguished gentleman being disorderly to anyone. I asked if he wanted to say anything before sentence. Foolish perhaps, but that's justice for you.

He did — and proceeded to launch into that well-known

monologue by the melancholic lord, Jaques, in William Shakespeare's *As You Like It*, again with multiple flourishes. 'All the world's a stage, And all the men and women merely players; They have their exits and their entrances.' And so on. And so on. Now I happen to know this piece and it would take a while to get to the 'Sans teeth, sans eyes, sans taste, sans everything'.

The police prosecutor was enjoying it. The lawyers were having a ball. Those in the public gallery were racking their brains for any poetry they knew to roll out when it was their turn.

He finally finished to applause from the back. It was clearly time to wrap this up. 'Sir, you are convicted and discharged. No other sentence. You are free to go.'

'My lady, I'm obliged,' and off he went.

Interruptions to the court day more often come in one of two more prosaic forms. The first, the fire alarm. So we all troop outside and wait for the fire department to establish that, no, it wasn't a fire but a prisoner in the cells who, tired of having nothing to do, blocked up the smoke alarms. Or possibly the same prisoner, still bored to tears, creates a steady dull thud with his feet on the cell bars that is intensely distracting and prolonged. Like an errant child you want to give away.

In the Family Court, the unexpected content of an affidavit can provide great opportunity for mirth, especially if written by a non-lawyer. There are many examples of women stating why they cannot identify their child's father, when asked. Some run into trouble, as evidenced by these US examples:

'So much about that night is a blur. The only thing that I remember for sure is that Delia Smith did a programme about eggs earlier in the evening. If I had stayed in and watched more TV, rather than going to the party at 8956 Miller Ave, mine might have remained unfertilized.'

Or this less elegant excuse: 'I am unsure as to the identity of the father of my baby, after all, like when you eat a can of beans, you can't be sure which one made you fart.'

I do like those examples which suggest some pressure has been exerted on a naive young woman. Like this one: 'I cannot tell you the name of Alleshia's dad as he informs me that to do so would blow his cover and have cataclysmic implications for the economy. I am torn between doing right by you and right by the country. Please advise.'

One day in a smaller court, an older building with lots of draughts and gaps in the floorboards, I was sitting at the bench, trying to decide which of the 18 stamps in front of me I should use, when, out of the corner of my eye, I spied a mouse. Not a large mouse, granted. In fact, Robbie Burns would call it 'a wee sleekit cowrin tim'rous beastie' kind of mouse.

I called it a direct challenge to my sanity, terrified of them as I am. The 'panic in *my* breastie' felt like a heart attack. A scream started to rise in my throat and I choked it off, only because if I let loose and jumped up on the bench, I knew it would forever define me.

I can see the headlines now, a permanent source of derision: 'Judge holds rodent in contempt'.

I took a hurried adjournment and fled.

11 On circuit

WHILE JUDGES WORK MOSTLY in their home court, they do travel to other smaller courts to do what is known as circuit work. There, resources are usually somewhat limited, sometimes with fewer security officers and decidedly less palatial chambers and facilities.

One judge travelled to a circuit court in her private car, rather than the usual court vehicle which wasn't available. She conducted a mediation conference with an angry man who spent a lot of the time swearing at his wife. At times, during the conference, the judge had to be very firm with him. At the end of the conference he stormed out.

About a quarter of an hour later, court staff rushed in, looking very serious. They told the judge the man had obviously damaged her car as there was a large dent in one side and numerous other dents elsewhere. It looked like it had been smashed quite seriously.

With as much judicial dignity as she could muster, she told them that was the normal state of her vehicle and she wasn't taking any responsibility for the dings because they were caused by her children.

If the particular court is a distance away, we stay for the week. Mike accompanies me. As a writer, all he needs is a laptop to keep him busy during the day.

Lunchtimes can be tricky. In a small town, it's awkward discovering you're in the same café as that angry parent you dealt with just an hour earlier. Most people give a judge a wide berth. Others want to use the opportunity to point out the errors of my judgment. Occasionally, it can be a pleasant encounter.

I remember sentencing a young man in a small-town court. He'd been convicted of burglary, a serious charge, and could have received a prison term. But the 'burg' was an opportunistic one by a bored teenager who was, by now, very remorseful and supported in court by his grandmother with whom he lived.

I had asked him what his dreams were. He talked about carpentry. I pointed out he'd never have the chance to pursue that if he kept nicking people's stuff. Moreover, he'd let his grandmother down and his behaviours had shamed her as well as him. He agreed with me, in a wobbly voice.

I stepped back from a prison sentence with police endorsement and imposed community work.

Later at lunchtime, I rounded a corner and there he was with his granny. He shook my hand and assured me he'd learned from what I'd said. His grandmother had the kind of fierce determination that suggested he would find his true values and make something of himself. For me, it was an emotional encounter.

In a different town, while doing circuit work, I had another chance meeting. This one started badly.

We were staying at a motel near town. It was our usual, and Mike and I were always welcomed by the owners. Before we settled in, they would give us their view of the town's current state of health. We'd hear about the bikies, the ones who were struggling, essentially the good, the bad and the little buggers.

Later in our room, I heard loud music, not a good sign early evening on a Sunday. After an hour, the beat of the bass got to me and I strolled across the road, intending to use my most measured voice, to see if the volume could be turned down a tad.

I was met with a 'fuck off' and various other expletives. Now as you may already have gathered, colourful language is common in court. Police read statements of fact with a straight face that belies the effing and blinding involved. Witnesses tell it like it is. Defendants think they'll upset the judge with a few expletives. It's water off the proverbial back. We've heard it all before.

So, on this occasion, I try to listen to find out if there's any point to the loud music. Turns out the occasion was her twenty-first birthday party. I look around at those lounging on a car, cans in hand. No presents or decorations. Just a general piss-up like any other night.

I go back to the motel and reflect on that to Mike. I think about my own twenty-first, the people, the gifts, the good food, and suddenly I feel very sad. I mourn for those who never know what it's like to feel special for all the right reasons, those who are feted and loved, who come to expect that on every birthday, never mind a twenty-first, there will be presents beautifully wrapped and cards spelling out how loved they are.

Time for action. So Mike and I go down to KFC, buy $50 worth of food and march back to the house with it. 'I just want to say happy birthday,' and we hand it over. They look gob-smacked. The birthday girl says, 'I'm sorry for swearing at you.' Strange that's the first thing she thinks of.

The music level is not mentioned, but 10 minutes after we've gone, we can't hear it.

She didn't know who I was and I wouldn't have wanted her to. These things can get complicated if she turns out to be one of the punters. Thankfully, I don't see her in court during the rest of my stint there.

That was some years ago now and I often think about her. What did 21 lead to? Those who are kicked from pillar to post and don't learn about the discipline necessary to build a career are starting way behind the rest of us. I was fortunate to have parents who loved me. As the oldest of five and the only girl, there were expectations to find my métier, to be the best I could be.

My parents came from Scotland in 1950 after they got married. They came to build a new life in a land free of the class system that dominated Great Britain.

My mother in particular often made the comparison between Scottish history, in which the English took control of a lot of Scottish land for their own entertainment, and what happened to Māori losing autonomy over their land, leaving them second-class citizens.

She tells the story of having an older Māori man to dinner with them when I was about 18 months old. Apparently, he watched me play and sometime during the course of the meal told Mum that, one day, I would be high up and people would look up to me.

Of course, later she took this to mean a sign of my acting chops, thinking I'd be up there on the stage. But when I was appointed to the bench, she told me that story for the first time, realising its meaning was elsewhere.

My mother has always been a very fey Scotswoman. She trusts her intuition. Maybe she passed that on to me.

I was sitting in court one morning. In smaller towns, lawyers are sometimes permitted to attend by telephone, to save travel costs for what may only be a brief court appearance.

At one such callover, I, and the lawyers present, were listening on the loudspeaker to the earnest submissions of a young male lawyer. His voice sounded tinny, like it was being delivered down a long metal tube. I had a hunch he might be in the toilet. Do I ask him to flush? Or am I going to make an idiot of myself if it's just a bad line?

My intuition said he was in the smallest room in the house and so I enquired politely if that were so. Indeed, I was right. He got a bollocking and the lawyers in front of me looked smug. *They* were in the right room.

Circuit work introduces a judge to a refreshingly wide variety of sectors of their community. There are the farmers arriving in their pickups with the dog in the back. They (the farmers not the dogs) clump into court in their gumboots and Swanndris wondering to themselves if the sheila up the front knows her stuff.

In other rural parts, where the crops are not primarily sheep, they arrive with dreads and wearing multicoloured muslin still looking a little spaced out at their dilemma and wondering if the chick up there is cool or not cool.

Despite the Ministry of Justice's wish for homogeneity among the various courtrooms of New Zealand, there are definitely nuances which define them — local colour if you will.

One rural courtroom which should remain anonymous was memorable for all the wrong reasons. The room housing the judge's chambers had the sign on the inside of the door, rather than the outside, which always struck me as strange. At least when the door was shut, I knew where I was. Off that room was the judge's bathroom, but no lock on the door and, even at a stretch, too far from the toilet to the door to keep a monitory hand out.

The most memorable feature, from an olfactory point of view, was the smell that gradually increased in intensity in the vague area where the judge usually sat. I know some wits would say, well, it would smell there, wouldn't it? It got worse and worse until it became unbearable. Further investigation led to the discovery of a dead animal under the floorboards. Payback from a possum.

If you're lucky at a court near the sea, you might go home with a snapper, courtesy of a court staffer who's been out in his boat and caught a few, or be offered some grapes from a registrar's garden. But one has to be careful about giving and receiving.

I recall being in a small court, hearing family matters, one grey wintry day. A grandmother was there to get an uncontested final parenting order for her six mokopuna who'd been with her for some time.

Neither Mum nor Dad could care for the children and they were nowhere to be seen. An order, as she told me, would ensure she could have some say if either parent ever wandered back and wanted to take one or more of the children.

Lawyer for the children described the grandmother's home as a very simple uncompleted dwelling that lacked some basic amenities but had loads of aroha.

I granted the order, but thought as I signed it off of the struggle she must have to put food on the table. I suddenly remembered a supermarket voucher in my bag, courtesy of a group I'd spoken to recently.

I adjourned, grabbed the voucher and asked the court registrar to give it to the grandmother who was just leaving court. 'Tell her it's from you,' I emphasised. It wouldn't do having it known a judge was handing out supermarket vouchers.

12 'Line 'em up and shoot 'em'

IT'S COMMON IN A BIG FAMILY for there to be a range of views about how society should be ordered. One of my brothers is an advocate of shoot first and ask questions afterwards. He'll often ask in a growly voice how many I put away today. Yes, all tough and uncompromising, but a marshmallow inside.

I think to myself, it's easier to be like that — to round 'em up and damn 'em to hell. I hear that view expounded on talkback, even in slightly more moderate tones, about longer sentences and harsher penalties, as if that will make a budding burglar stop and think twice at the gate. Research in the United States indicates that harsher sentences are not the deterrent that some suggest.[18]

It's an understandable reaction too from a segment of society who see things in black and white. It's not their problem, it's those bleep bleep (add your own particular prejudice here).

Comments are punctuated with 'they should' as if to say if only 'they' could get their shit together, we'd all be okay. It's outrageous to suggest it might be our problem, since we raised our kids to be decent clean-living people who never see the inside of a courtroom, never mind a jail.

Those views spew forth over coffee, on radio, Facebook and Twitter. It's easier than reflecting on how we got to the stage where Māori make up 52 per cent of our prisons, despite being only 16 per cent of the population, or why 75 per cent of women inmates are sexual and/or family abuse survivors.[19]

As long as we stand outside the problem, we remove ourselves from any solutions.

What drives crime and how do we turn around these statistics? Is it *our* problem because we all live together on these islands?

Let's start with a normal day in the criminal court where we judges see a procession of people and sometimes learn a bit about their lives. The police will read out the summary of facts in a plain and unadorned fashion.

The probation report will give some background to the defendant's circumstances, their family, work, medical history.

The victim will tell the court in a statement how the offending made them feel, including the emotional and financial cost.

The defendant's lawyer might add some other pertinent information accompanied by evidence, talk of remorse or produce letters of support from the community.

Put all that together and you have some, but not necessarily a complete, picture of what led to the offending and whether it was premeditated or opportunistic.

Is this an essentially bad person who should go to prison for as long as the law allows to keep the rest of us safe? Is there such a creature as an essentially bad person anyway?

My husband recalls a stint he did at Auckland's Paremoremo prison while he was a chaplain there. He reckons no more than 5 per cent of the men there were really bad, which means 95 per cent of them could be rehabilitated to a more productive life.

I'm fascinated by the different approach to punishment

demonstrated in Scandinavian countries like Norway. There, one maximum security prison focuses almost exclusively on rehabilitation. There are no security cameras or barred windows. Yes, the time must be served, but statistics show their recidivism rate is significantly lower than in the rest of the world: 20 per cent compared to 67 per cent in the United States over two and three years of leaving prison.[20]

It should be obvious I'm not a fan of the 'lock 'em up and throw away the key' brigade. If we have the resources, and that's often a challenge, I believe redemption is possible.

When I've heard it said there's no budget for another residential men's programme or drug abuse recovery facility, I think how amazing that we were able to commandeer millions and millions of dollars to fight a pandemic. I also think of the annual cost to the country of family abuse at $4 to $7 billion. Can we afford not to spend that money? We're already paying the price.

I read an interesting book called *The Tipping Point* by Malcolm Gladwell. In it, he explored how a product, event or small idea can suddenly catch the public imagination and spread like wildfire. We've seen it with the #MeToo movement, the events following George Floyd's death and the call for the toppling of many statues.

But what's the tipping point for these events? Why is it sparked then and not earlier in history? Is it simply because its time has come?

Take the case of Hush Puppies, described in his book.[21] Until about 1994, they were brushed suede shoes that the sartorially minded wouldn't have been seen dead in. Then they became fashionable to a certain set and sales took off. How then, Gladwell asks, does a $30 pair of shoes go from a handful of downtown Manhattan hipsters and designers to every mall in America in the space of two years?

A change of heart is possible. People can radically transform their behaviours or beliefs if given the right impetus to do so. I'm not just talking about criminals (or Hush Puppies) but those of a more prejudiced bent too. 'Change the way you look at things and the things you look at will change', as the old saying goes.

What would it take for a tipping point to be reached on our approach to crime?

What would happen if we collectively had compassion not condemnation, if we had people queueing up to help adult prisoners read and write, or sent out our extra possessions to Women's Refuge, or gave practical support to organisations like the Howard League who work with those newly out of prison.

What would it be like if judgmental chit-chat withered and died? If kindness really was the national mantra?

If we're passing judgment on a person from our armchair, we never really confront the lawlessness. We generalise, write them off.

Restorative justice is a concept which puts the offender and victim in the same room, where hard questions are raised by the victim and the wrongdoer's shame is held up to the light for scrutiny. There is now a statutory requirement for a judge to consider a restorative justice conference before sentencing.

Sometimes it's not appropriate, but when it happens genuinely, it can be transformative for both sides. It's a powerful process and one that our society, hungry for revenge and punishment, could learn from.

In 2012, I spoke at a book launch. Chris Marshall had written a book called *Compassionate Justice*.[22] In it, he took two biblical parables, the Prodigal Son and the Good Samaritan, and applied notions of restorative justice to each.

The Prodigal Son is the story of a young man who goes to his father asking for his inheritance to spend now. The father obliges and the young man goes off and has a high old time. But then he runs out of money and is reduced to a job feeding pigs. For a Jew to feed pigs, which were seen as unclean, was to reach rock bottom. He thinks, maybe I could live on the scraps my father throws out, and he journeys to his father.

When the father sees him, he offers forgiveness and acceptance, and welcomes him back into the family. This doesn't go down well with the older brother, who has laboured away, never receiving *his* inheritance or even a goat to celebrate and here's the father laying on a feast for someone so unworthy of it.

The older son wanted retributive justice. The father offered restorative justice.

Retribution is payback. Restoration is remedial.

It needs to be said that mere attendance at a restorative justice conference is not automatically going to result in a lesser sentence. While the judge must take such attendance into account, it's what goes on there that's important. Where both the offender and victim can effect some change that benefits *both* parties, then, in my view, justice is really done. Sure, the offender still has to face the judge and be sentenced, but that is almost the lesser part of it all.

A demand for longer sentences may win votes at election time, but it won't stop crime or even reduce it. The 'three strikes' legislation was brought into effect in 2010 with the Sentencing and Parole Reform Act. It is aimed at habitual offenders and provides that, for serious offences such as sexual assault or robbery, a convicted person is given a warning as a first strike. Those convicted of a second qualifying offence are required to serve the actual sentence imposed by the judge. On the third occasion the maximum sentence is imposed without parole, unless the judge considers that sentence to be manifestly unjust.

There is no evidence such laws have done any more than institutionalise criminals and ensure they are even more ill prepared eventually for life outside the prison doors. In the years since the three strikes legislation was passed, crime statistics show few changes attributable to the law.[23]

Isn't it time we tried another way to punish, one that is coupled with a greater focus on rehabilitation, so a person can pay their debt to society and go on to contribute usefully something other than a life of crime?

To those who clamour for revenge, for harsher sentencing, for retribution, I say if that is the society we want, we are in danger of losing our humanity, and if we lose that, what is left?

13 Judged by your peers

FIRST, A DISCLAIMER. As a judge I undertook criminal matters in the summary jurisdiction and judge-alone trials. But I never did any jury trials. I would have left out this chapter except that the role of the juror is so important in our judicial system and the history of what jurors have gotten up to is so fascinating that I decided its inclusion was warranted. Besides, my colleagues and others have provided some good tales which bear repeating.

The concept of juries has been around since before Socrates' trial in 399 BC. Socrates was charged with impiety or, put simply, having a lack of reverence for the gods and the dead who had gone before. Five hundred good (male) citizens of Athens served as his jurors. They didn't all have to agree. At the end, 280 voted to convict him, while 220 said not guilty.

Socrates, on hearing the verdict, was allowed to speak on the proposed sentence, apparently a common practice then. It's said he unwisely mocked the jurors and 80 of the not-guilty lot changed their verdict to guilty as a result. His sentence? Death. Socrates opted to drink hemlock.

I.F. Stone, an American journalist, wrote *The Trial of*

Socrates in 1988.[24] He noted that Socrates acted more like
a picador trying to enrage a bull than a defendant trying to
mollify a jury and concluded the probable reason was that
Socrates was ready, at 71, to die.

The Normans first introduced juries to England. They
consisted of collections of neighbours assembled to answer
questions on oath. Not just any neighbour and never women;
they were men of standing who owned property. Until the
nineteenth century, they made decisions based on their
knowledge of people or the case.

Today we would know them as witnesses. They certainly
weren't impartial, and it wasn't until the 1800s that jurors
were expected to be non-partisan about the case they were
hearing.

On Sunday, 14 August 1670, Quakers William Penn and
William Mead were preaching to a small group of about 30
in London. They did so quietly, but in the spirit of the times
they were charged with 'unlawful and tumultuous assembly'.
The jury could not reach a verdict, despite going out four
times. The judge was getting frustrated at this and ordered
a unanimous verdict, saying, 'I will have a positive verdict
or you shall starve for it.' And starve he meant! No food, no
drink. And to make it worse, not even a chamber pot.

That was enough to produce action of a kind and the
jury returned with a unanimous 'not guilty' verdict. Our not
so impartial judge was incensed and fined each juror and
directed them to prison until they had paid.

The jury foreman appealed, and the Appeal Court agreed
that a jury must be indisputably responsible for their verdict,
free from any threats by the judge.

If juries lacked independence before then, they certainly
earned it thereafter.

A nineteenth-century trial by jury for murder was notable
not so much for the jury, although they reached their verdict
in an incredible 35 minutes. What happened after that was
equally astonishing and might possibly be endorsed by the

string-'em-up brigade today. The man was hanged before a crowd of several thousand people. The judge, who would probably belong to the same brigade, directed the hanging and the body to be dissected and anatomised. The surgeon cut off and dried the murderer's skin and used it to bind a copy of the trial transcript as a book. If you're interested, you can see the book on display at a museum in Suffolk.[25]

On a lighter note, just 40 years later in the United States, the rough and tumble town of Laramie in Wyoming found a way to address the Wild West anarchy that had prevailed there. Women in Wyoming Territory had gained the vote in December 1869. It was seen as a progressive move. The question of women being jurors arose. Many were opposed. Others felt it would bring a more genteel note to the court and even help clean up the town. The judge was in favour and so on 7 March 1870 six women were seated as jurors, against lawyers' objections. They reportedly did a fine job. But it was two steps forward and a few back when a subsequent judge prohibited women jurors and, with one exception, that remained the position in Wyoming until 1950.

Anyway, enough of the history lesson. As with all things, practices evolve and change. The notion that any jury members might be partisan in some way or that the judge had preconceived ideas about the outcome has been relegated to the dinosaurs.

But there is one unique jury that was, on only one occasion, empanelled in New Zealand.

The story occurred in 1883. Phoebe Veitch had three children by three different men by the time she was 20. Her husband was declared bankrupt and he took off soon after, leaving Phoebe to work as a seamstress and to take in other people's washing to make ends meet. All the while she was looking after her three children and blind mother. Phoebe also had serious health issues which were identified after her death as syphilis.

She was found guilty of child murder by a conventional

jury. Her four-year-old daughter Flossy drowned in flood waters and Phoebe's explanation for the death changed as police enquiries intensified.

The *Southland Times* of 3 May 1883 described the next step. 'His Honour the Chief Justice assumed the black cap and sentenced the prisoner to death.'

Here's where it got interesting. Phoebe was pregnant, her lawyer said, so the judge empanelled a jury of matrons, not nurses but respectable married women. Their task was to determine whether Phoebe was telling the truth.

Now although we live in simpler times where peeing on a strip will tell you after a few minutes if you're pregnant, life was not so straightforward then.

After five minutes the jury returned, asking for medical assistance as they couldn't determine the pregnancy. A doctor was brought in, but he couldn't help. Perhaps that was not so surprising then as it was midwives who dealt with pregnancy and birth not, in the main, doctors.

Eventually the matrons reached a verdict. Yes, Phoebe was pregnant. That saved her from the death penalty and her sentence was commuted to life in prison.

Phoebe had successfully 'pleaded her belly' as the medieval term was known.

Today our legal system views a jury as part of the democratic process. They comprise members of the public drawn from all walks of life. As such, they bring a diverse range of perspectives, personal experience and knowledge to bear on a case. Their task is to listen to the evidence and reach a verdict.

We don't know what goes on in the jury room and rely on anecdotal stories that filter out from time to time.

In one case, the jury retired to consider their verdict. A confident woman announced that she was best placed to be foreperson and was duly elected. Then she declared to all, 'Of course, we all know he's guilty.' That might have been the end of it were it not for the careful deliberations of all the jurors. Verdict? Not guilty.

My mother recalls being on a jury hearing an attempted rape charge. She had not been looking forward to performing her civic duty and marched to the jury box with a 'hang him high' look. Defence counsel let her go.

The jury were shown a book of photos. Mum turned them this way and that and couldn't make head nor tail of them. She thought she could make out flowers, but being a keen gardener was worried she was imposing her own world view rather than being the careful independent juror she had been called to be.

Her confusion was mirrored on the faces of the other jurors and eventually the judge stepped in. Turned out the photos belonged to a completely different trial. The jury was dismissed, and the trial had to be reconvened at a later date.

Juries see photos and exhibits and hear evidence that can be deeply personal or gruesome. In one murder trial, the defence lawyer attempted to argue before the trial began that the photos of the dead woman should not be shown to the jury. She had been hacked to death with a knife and the photos were particularly grisly. The prosecutor argued they should be shown.

The judge listened closely. Then he gave his decision, talking about how robust juries are these days, used to film and television depicting all kinds of scenes. He assured defence counsel the jury could handle it.

The jury were empanelled and the trial began. First up was the police photographer with the photos. A copy was handed out to each jury member.

One man ran from the jury box into the jury room and refused, despite prompting, to come out. Another juror burst into tears. And a third started squealing.

The judge conceded defeat and called for an adjournment. Defence counsel said not a word.

Jurors don't always get it right either. One memorable story comes from Stephen Pile's *The Book of Heroic*

Failures[26] (which gives you a clue). In a trial the complainant was asked what the defendant said he would like to do to her. She blushed and was coy about repeating the words. The judge suggested she write it down, which she duly did. The note was then passed to the jury. One juror had nodded off in all this, so when an attractive juror elbowed him and handed him the note, he read it, winked at her and put it in his pocket.

Jurors are human. They don't sit back, listen to all the evidence and then assess it at the end. They weigh it up as they go. According to a *New York Times* article on jurors, research suggests that a juror's unspoken assumption about human nature forms a powerful part of their final verdict.

Which makes sense when you think about it. We all come from different backgrounds, have different experiences of life and see the world through our own lens of attitudes, beliefs and prejudices. So, when confronted with a large Māori defendant, covered in tattoos, whom we're told is a gang member, discrimination creeps in as surely as the sun sets in the west.

Whenever I talk to people about courts and the jury system, invariably the conversation turns to how someone can get out of jury service, or how it interferes with their working life. The idea that they might be performing an important civic duty doesn't feature in the discussion, yet, apart from voting, it's one of the few times in our lives when we are asked to exercise our responsibility as citizens.

We all want a fair and impartial justice system, but we baulk at making that happen. Sure, the money for jurors is not great, starting at $31 plus expenses for half a day, but seen as community engagement it shifts the focus to the bigger picture in our lives. Let's face it, there are not many times these days when we are asked to do something for the greater societal good.

Employers are supposed to pay staff who serve on juries in New Zealand. If they fail to do so, they can be held in contempt of court. While an employer has no legal obligation to top up an employee's lost wages (unless such provision is contained in their employment contract), it's a mean-spirited employer who wouldn't do so.

The juror's attendance fee hasn't risen since 2004, but the rationale of Amy Adams when she was Justice Minister was that the fee is intended to be a thank you to jurors for their service, not a wage replacement.[27] Which is fine as long as a wage earner isn't seriously out of pocket for doing the right thing. Jurors are nervous enough about the prospect of sitting on a jury, without the financial impact.

The nerves can lead a prospective juror to get it all wrong, as occurred in the following exchange:

Nervous possible juror: Judge I'd like to be excused from the jury because my wife is about to become pregnant.

Lawyer: Your Honour, he does not mean his wife is about to become pregnant. He means she is about to deliver.

His Honour: He is excused. In either event, he should be present.

If you persist and ignore all I say about civic duty, I'd say your best bet at getting out of jury service would be to claim you are psychic and already know the verdict. Therefore, you couldn't possibly remain impartial.

14 Court etiquette

A YOUNG WOMAN, about 18, came into court one day with her mother. She was there for an order declaring that her ex was the father of her child. She had filed her application only because Work and Income required to know and have it confirmed who the father was so they could pursue him for child support. She was receiving a benefit, so it was the state's way of recouping some of that cost.

He had been served with the application but probably decided it wasn't worth fighting since he knew he was the father, so no defence had been filed.

Her child was young. Maybe she was putting her mammary glands to good use. They were on full display this particular day, only partially concealed in a tank top. Indeed, it was a garment designed to reveal — a lot.

Now I am all in favour of breastfeeding mums, but there was no baby in sight and she was drawing attention for all the wrong reasons. Our male court taker had a slightly glazed and fixed stare as he kept his eyes on the opposite wall.

I needed to make a call here. 'Ms [whoever she was], you are dressed inappropriately for court. Do you have a jacket or jersey?'

'Ah, yeah.'

'Well, put it on.'

This was no Marilyn Monroe aware of the effect of her swelling bosom on others, but a very young naive woman who probably dressed like that every day, whatever the occasion, court, wedding, supermarket.

The sad thing is she was accompanied by her mother, whose neckline was only a little higher and who seemed totally oblivious to my concerns.

Another judge encountered a visitor to the Youth Court one day, a young woman of 19 or so who arrived wearing a voluminous pink dressing gown. She bounced into court, seemingly unconcerned about her garb. The judge took her to task and asked why she hadn't got dressed before coming to court. She looked surprised at the rebuke. 'Well, I didn't have time,' as if it were obvious. It was, by then, 11.30 a.m. When the judge sternly suggested that next time she should wear clothes, she completely missed the reprimand and cheerfully said, 'Okey-dokey.'

Etiquette has been described as the customary code of polite behaviour in society. In the court setting, it means a number of things.

Short skirts and low-cut tops are frowned on for lawyers, though the colour of your shoes is no longer a matter of judicial comment as it once was. 'I can't see you,' said one judge to a male lawyer wearing, shock and horror, brown shoes. It wasn't a comment on the judge's eyesight but an indication of how offended the judge was, and his refusal to hear anything more until the hapless lawyer changed his footwear.

Even today, the Law Society sets out the expected dress code for lawyers. Black shoes are stipulated for the High Court, Court of Appeal and Supreme Court. They are not mentioned in the District Court list, but that doesn't mean jandals are acceptable. I note it's not okay for lawyers to bring coffee into court without permission. No one ever asked me if their takeaway flat white sitting on their table was acceptable.

Court etiquette says lawyers should bow to the judge, refrain from interrupting them — and that probably goes for arguing as well — and be polite to other lawyers and court staff. Don't smoke or take photos. Don't eat food or wear a T-shirt depicting offensive slogans. Those T-shirts that your dodgy uncle gave you for Christmas proclaiming, 'Ask me about my explosive diarrhoea' and 'Masturbation never breaks your heart' should definitely stay in the drawer.

Lawyers, police and defendants should address the judge as 'Your Honour'.

For male judges it's often 'sir'. For female judges it's often 'sir', though that's usually because a lawyer forgets themselves. I once threatened to call a male lawyer Mrs if he addressed me once more as sir. 'Ma'am' is also acceptable, though many defendants, having heard this from their lawyers, often mistake what they hear and call me 'Mum'.

We women judges have also been called your majesty (which went down well), your worship, aunty (which I liked as I don't have a living aunty), and whaea (mother, aunt) as well as the other less-pleasant designations. One of my colleagues was appointed to a court where they had never had a female judge. She was called 'sir' so often that she said in desperation one day, 'Please! Is my chin particularly hairy today?'

Court etiquette is about maintaining a certain standard, not only because a judge is present but because behind the judge on the wall is a coat of arms depicting Māori and the Crown. It's a symbol of our sovereignty and reflects our bicultural origins, showing a Pākehā woman and a Māori male.

We have become more casual as a society from the days of men in suits and hats and ladies wearing gloves. A defendant is as likely to turn up to court in a hoodie. But it's not the particular clothing I care about so much, though I also draw the line at singlets and sunglasses. I have been caught out once by sunglasses. A lawyer came into court wearing what I thought were spectacles. The longer he was there, the darker the glasses became. I was about to call him out on his sunnies when I realised they were prescription glasses which automatically darken when you're inside.

Etiquette can be an attitude and there are standards of behaviour that everyone in the court should adhere to. The lawyer who addressed the judge as 'Yo, judge' back in 2009[28] drew the ire of the Attorney-General, speaking in Parliament, calling for a higher standard at the criminal bar. Fair enough too.

Lawyers are bound by rules of conduct that require them to act professionally, protect their client's interests and carry out their duty of fidelity to the court. Specifically, a lawyer has an absolute duty of honesty to the court and must not mislead or deceive the court. A lawyer cannot approach the bench without the judge's permission. Nor can they leave court if they are the last lawyer left in court, without permission.

They begin their submission with 'If Your Honour pleases . . .' They refer to opposing counsel as 'my learned friend'. They must sit immediately when another lawyer gets to their feet.

To some, these might seem like anachronistic practices, a throwback to a bygone era, but they are part of the language of the court. Every group has its vernacular, and the language of the law is no different. If that language sounds to you, a visitor to the court, like it's irrelevant or even weird, just remember it has layers of meaning.

When the lawyer rises to their feet to object to where the judge is heading with an idea, saying, 'With the greatest of respect Your Honour,' you know that they think that your idea is pretty stupid. But couched like that, only those in the know are aware the lawyer thinks the judge is off in Noddy Land. It's subtle.

The same goes for that lovely phrase I've heard so often, 'I'd invite Your Honour to reconsider . . .' Pull up, pull up judge, before you hit the choppy waters of a completely dopey decision.

I've watched the dance so often as each tries to steer a way through the etiquette of polite submissions between a judge and lawyer. The undercurrent goes something like this:

'That's the most inane submission I've ever heard.'

'Well, if you weren't a dumb Family Court judge, you'd know it's got merit.'

'Pul-eeze, you wouldn't know merit if it bit you on the bottom.'

'Fine. Do your worst. I'll appeal.'

'Oh, play it dirty, eh?'

For the most part, lawyers have been, in my experience, respectful and discreet, notwithstanding the above.

Generally, it's not the lawyers breaching the etiquette of the court. It's those in their spaghetti strap tops. We don't want to see your belly button in court. Save it for the beach.

15 'So, what do you do for a living?'

WHEN OUR FUTURE SON-IN-LAW first met our daughter and learned her mother worked at the court, he assumed for a long time she was a secretary. After all, why would you think she was a judge, right? We've teased him a lot about that in the years since.

The twenty-first century has not yet ushered in an era of men and women on an equal footing, whatever their roles might be. Take law, for instance. Women make up more than half of law students and have done for many years. By the time you get to the bench, though, women judges comprise 32.3 per cent of the judiciary in New Zealand.[29]

Addressing the imbalance is not easy.

You'd be forgiven for thinking that equality came long ago, given that women first got the vote in New Zealand in 1893, well ahead of most other democracies such as Britain and the United States. And that Ethel Benjamin was New Zealand's first woman lawyer way back in September 1897.

It was 1933 when Elizabeth McCombs became the first female Member of Parliament, representing Lyttelton, and she was followed by a string of women through the 1940s and 50s.

The Second World War saw women worldwide entering the workforce in factories and on farms or working as drivers and nurses and other roles. However, women were expected to relinquish those roles after the war in favour of their menfolk returning from battle. It was back to the kitchen for another decade until again societal expectations started to shift in favour of women seeking greater personal freedom and equal rights.

Since the 1970s, when I started work, I have seen a forward-backwards dance which some 50 years later leaves me worried about what still needs to be achieved before we can say, women and men alike, that we are partners in business, commerce and the home.

Why did it take until 2018 for women to finally comprise the majority of school principals in New Zealand when, for decades, teaching had been a female-dominated profession?

Why do women comprise only 24 per cent of members of boards in New Zealand?

Why is it many women are the cooks in the home, yet make up a fraction of New Zealand chefs? It's complicated I know, but when we see men in leadership roles, we make the often-unspoken assumption it's because men belong there.

I've lost count of the number of functions I've attended where that casual question comes up: 'And what do you do for a living?' When I say I'm a judge, it's sometimes like admitting to being a tax inspector.

Where does the conversation go from there? The brave ones take a stab at it and want to know the details. Others, usually men, can't get their heads around it and make a joke about whether we've met before. But a real discussion about our respective careers is usually off the table.

When my husband and I have been away on circuit and the hotel or motel knows that Judge Riddell has made a reservation, 99 per cent of the time they look to Mike as the likely judge. Same thing with taxi drivers.

When court staff from around the country write to me

and don't know who I am they automatically assume Judge Riddell is male.

Don't get me wrong. I don't have some innate need to be recognised or feted. But it's interesting that even among Generations X, Y and Z, they still haven't got their heads around the idea that this job, or most jobs, can be done by a woman. When we ask who the doctor, plumber or pilot is, we inevitably mentally assign the wrong gender pronoun.

Since I've retired, people almost never ask me what I did for a living before retirement. My husband is a writer, so his job simply goes on.

As for me, well, I was probably a secretary or office worker, worthy enough occupations but not ones you would want to start up a conversation about.

I once met a couple well into their seventies and asked him what first attracted the man to his wife. He said it was her skill in landing a plane straight down the runway with minimal bumps. Turns out they were both pilots and had devoted their lives to aviation. He always said she was the better pilot!

So how do we shift perceptions about who people are and what they do?

Living in the countryside, it's easy to assume the husband is the farmer, but I've learned from experience that both husband and wife farm, milk, do the calving and round up the sheep. That first came home to me years ago when we had a crib at Hindon, inland from Dunedin. Our neighbours were farmers; she was a vegetarian who raised coloured sheep. Both were equally farmers, equally committed to the land and lifestyle.

I'm at a cocktail function, about to give a speech on being a judge. There's a mix of audience, lawyers, Rotary members, businesspeople and the public. A man approaches me, and we chat. He's heard a judge is speaking tonight. 'Yes,' I murmur.

'Well, I hope he's not one of these liberal twats who

doesn't know his arse from his elbow.'

'So, what do you do for a living?', hoping to deflect him.

'Oh, I'm an engineer. Seen a lot of these judges in court when I've given evidence. You'd think they'd know right at the outset when some chump doesn't have a case. But no, on it goes for four or five days. Still, pays the bills. I'm happy to talk. And you, what do you do?'

I'm just a liberal twat.

'Well, actually I'm the speaker.' He pales. 'And, I've got a fairly good idea of the significant difference between my arse and my elbow.' He heads for the bar.

I would be lying if I said that judges never make these assumptions. I remember when I was newly appointed and attending the triennial conference for judges. On the last day, we checked out of our accommodation and headed outside. I started to put my bag in the back of the taxi van ordered for the judges. One judge blustered up to me and said loudly, 'This van is reserved for judges.' He could not conceive of the idea that I might be one.

Sometimes at public occasions, I say I'm a film director. That is true after all.

In 2009, I directed the film adaptation of Mike's first novel *The Insatiable Moon*. The film was to be a big-budget one with a Scottish director and a cast that included Timothy Spall. Like all films, it was years in the planning and subject to the vagaries of the Film Commission who were keen, then they weren't, then they. . .

Anyway, when the funding fell over and the Scottish director walked, the UK producer and Mike asked if I would consider directing. They knew I had a long holiday planned for the end of that year, so I could watch the film being made.

I had already been involved in auditioning the cast and had gathered some of New Zealand's finest actors. We had Ian Mune, Sara Wiseman, Greg Johnson and, in the lead role, Rawiri Paratene of *Whale Rider* fame. I knew the script inside out. I could do this. It was my first feature film.

I had already directed a short film before becoming a judge. It was called *Cake Tin* and we entered it, on the spur of the moment, in the Moondance Film Festival. When we were shortlisted, we decided to attend the ceremony in Hollywood and were blown away when our little black-and-white film was awarded the Sandcastle Award for best film by a male and female team.

Fast forward to late 2009, and off we went to Auckland where most of the filming was on location in parts of Ponsonby. I had a superb director of photography, Tom Burstyn, who treated me like a seasoned pro. The four weeks of shooting took us up to Christmas.

At one point we were loaned a residential boarding house for the scenes about psychiatric residents. The owner took most of the residents away on holiday, but a couple wandered back and took to walking in front of the camera as we were about to shoot. I asked one gentleman if he'd like to be in our movie. 'Oh no love,' he replied. 'I'm already broadcasting on 24 channels.'

The crew found it amusing that they had a judge for a director. I'm not sure they knew what to make of me at times, especially when I threatened jail or community work if a scene wasn't dressed right.

The plot centred on a psychiatric patient who believed he was the Second Son of God. It was based on Arthur, a real live character who would visit Mike at our church in Ponsonby and ask him to read the parts of the Bible where it says Jesus is the Son of God. Then he'd shake his head and murmur, 'Boy he's going to be in trouble.'

We wrapped up on budget and on time and then managed to raise the finance for post-production. The film was first released at the Auckland Film Festival in 2010 and had a season in the UK as well.

I found it interesting when a judge would ring me and say they had seen the film, then add, 'It's *really good*,' as if they expected it to be rubbish.

We were very proud of our film, which was awarded best actor and best supporting actor at the following year's New Zealand Film Awards. I felt pleased, too, that I had another string to my bow, even if I didn't intend to abandon law and branch out into the mercurial world of filmmaking.

Frank Capra, an Italian-American film director, once said there are no rules in filmmaking. Only sins. And the cardinal sin is dullness. Whatever our film was, it wasn't dull.

When we ask someone, 'So what do you do for a living?', the answer is going to enable us to compartmentalise them in some way.

So, you're a teacher, you know how to cope with kids in a classroom.

Ah, you're a nurse, you don't mind the sight of blood.

Oh, you're on a sickness benefit. Well, I must get another drink.

Sometimes when I've said I'm a judge, people look guilty . . .

16 The poverty trap

NEW ZEALAND'S OFFICIAL rate of child poverty places 23 per cent of children below the poverty line.[30] That means children living in substandard housing, not having enough food and experiencing a whole raft of health issues. The rates for Māori and Pasifika are higher than the national average.

The poverty trap means for those caught by it, there is little chance of escape to a better life. House prices in New Zealand push the dream of ownership out of reach for many. Incomes for basic jobs remain at the same level and many jobs have, over the past 30 years, simply disappeared.

Care workers in retirement homes and nurses in hospitals are by no means at the top of the income stream. But as we have seen recently with Covid-19, it was *those* people who proved to be the essential workers, vital to keeping life in New Zealand going, even while the rest of us were in lockdown. It turned on its head the notion of what was vital.

Turns out the rubbish collector was, and the stockbroker wasn't.

The poverty trap has implications for those who go through the court system.

Take Jimmy, for example. He's never had much of a record except for some youthful misdemeanours involving alcohol. Now he has a partner and three kids. He manages to get a job on the new motorway construction, bringing in a regular income. Life's good.

The motorway gets completed and he can't find any other labouring work. Times get tough.

In desperation one day, he steals some items from the supermarket and, while that would normally be treated as a minor offence warranting diversion, he compounds the problem by lashing out at the supermarket security guard, who's hospitalised as a result. Now he's up on an aggravated assault charge and subject to bail conditions.

To make matters worse, the house the family were staying in courtesy of an uncle is no longer theirs. The uncle wants to put his children in there, and quickly.

Our Jimmy doesn't know about tenancy rights and the uncle certainly isn't going to let on about his legal obligations to his tenants. So, the family is on the move, initially to a friend's garage. While they are there, the police visit. Seems Jimmy forgot that his bail conditions require him to live at an approved address and not to move without police consent. He's breached that and he's angry. Shortly after that, he's under arrest and in the cells.

His partner wants to come and see him when he's next in court, but they have no car and the bus service is patchy at best.

One of the kids has asthma and the partner must toss up whether to see Jimmy or take the child to the doctor. She opts for the latter.

The following day when Jimmy appears in court after his night in the cells there's no partner and children to greet him from the public gallery. Jimmy's hurt and he's more than a bit miffed that a shoplifting offence has ballooned out of control.

Boundaries were not something Jimmy knew anything about when growing up. In his case, it was safer to sleep under the house than in it. He was knocked around, went hungry and attended more schools than he could remember. As a result, his reading and writing skills are shaky at best.

There has been some light in Jimmy's life, though, and that was firstly his partner. She took him in hand and showed him a love he'd never known before. They wanted a family and, three children later, Jimmy's life was looking pretty good — until he lost his job. Then the old patterns of behaviour came back to haunt him, lashing out rather than reasoning.

Jimmy's life could now go one of two ways. He could find a house and a job, and his circumstances could be faithfully recorded by his probation officer, evincing sympathy from the judge who will sentence him. Jimmy and the security guard meet in a restorative justice conference. As a result, they see each other as more than offender and victim. Jimmy learns something about justice tempered with mercy that he has never encountered before. Change is slow, but with support and the leniency of a judge who sees more than a man handy with his fists, Jimmy serves a term of intensive supervision with conditions attached. He never sees the inside of a courtroom again.

The other route could be that unemployment and homelessness continue to beset him. The pressure produces cracks in the relationship. Jimmy lashes out at his partner, attempting to strangle her. She flees with the children to a women's refuge. She comes close to losing the children to the state when Oranga Tamariki, the Ministry for Children, respond to an anonymous notification from a neighbour who heard the violence. Now, she is on her own with the kids, trying to provide them with the basics of life. She has not much in the way of support networks and even less to start a home and furnish it.

The poverty trap comes in many guises.

Often it's intergenerational, so a child growing up with a father and grandfather who've never had steady work doesn't get to see Dad getting up early, making his lunch, coming home after a hard day, knowing that Dad does this to put food on the table.

He might not realise that Mum goes out after his bedtime to clean offices and motels. Or that she volunteers at the local op shop while he is at school, in exchange for some free clothes.

Our society majors on consumerism, creating a need for things that are, at best, luxury items not essentials. And it's not only the rich who hunger for stuff. The poor do too. Only difference is the rich can satiate their hunger easily. The poor go into hock for the big TV or the PlayStation.

There are laws in New Zealand designed to protect consumers when they buy goods on credit or borrow money. But who knows about the Credit Contracts and Consumer Finance Act or thinks to go to a Community Law Centre when they find the money they borrowed has now incurred a whopping interest rate, or that washing machine turned out to have a dodgy pedigree?

It's not only household goods or extras that see people applying to loan sharks. Some borrow to meet their daily living costs.

In 2013, a TV3 news investigation revealed an unregistered South Auckland finance company was charging up to 450 per cent interest on short-term loans and threatened to 'get dirty' if they weren't paid.[31] As the Child Poverty Action Group (CPAG) reported at the time: 'The Government says it isn't illegal for companies to charge exorbitant interest rates on loans.'[32]

Legislative changes may have knocked that particular evil on the head. The most recent credit law changes will, for instance, limit the total of the loan owed to twice the amount originally borrowed, thus preventing the extortionate interest-rate scenario described above.

So how would the Jimmy in our story fare in the public eye if he couldn't get either a job or house?

As CPAG's 2019 report noted, 'A large proportion of the New Zealand public despise the poor and especially those on benefits.'[33] There's scorn that they are bludgers, that they shouldn't have children and, if immigrants, that they should go back to where they came from.

But the problem isn't dependency. It's poverty.

When I left school and started work in 1970, there were almost no unemployed.

Imagine that!

Even those who didn't have a skill could always get a job, at the Railways for instance. Others could go 'seagulling', approaching the wharves for work for a day. There was factory work in the car industry. Now it's all done by robots. That's also happened with breweries and canning. Automation is rife, in rural and urban sectors.

Many apprenticeships have also gone. Evening classes to help people upskill at a moderate cost have ceased. And we all know that economic growth alone hasn't adequately addressed poverty. Look at the trickle-down theory of economics. The trickle has mostly gushed upwards.

I'm not against progress. I am simply noting the change in employment options has seen a rise of the managerial class. People are separated from doing something for which they see a result. People need to work, to produce something.

Granted how we earn money and produce something will have to change, but we need to take everyone along with us. As Alvin Toffler prophetically wrote, the illiterate of the twenty-first century will not be those who cannot read and write, but those who cannot learn, unlearn, and relearn.

For now, with the best will in the world, some families cannot pay all their bills, even if they do have jobs. I have seen breakdowns of income and expenditure in Family Court documents and I wonder sometimes how people manage.

As long as some New Zealand families are locked in poverty, then the whole of our society is impoverished.

As Nelson Mandela put it, poverty is not an accident. Like slavery and apartheid, it is created, and it can be removed by the actions of human beings.

17 'I've never been here before'

PICTURE IF YOU WILL a middle-class couple sitting uncomfortably in court with their teenage son. The public gallery is packed, and they are wedged next to a young Māori woman who has a wriggling baby on her lap and two school-aged children playing at her feet. For the whānau, the courtroom is as familiar as home. Not so for the couple and son.

They all wait, through the morning and into the afternoon. Everyone has been given the direction to be at court at 10 a.m., but it's now creeping towards three o'clock. Eventually the young man is called up. He stands in the dock, looking very downcast. His parents edge forward in their seats, their anxiety palpable.

Their son has been charged with possession of methamphetamine for supply, specifically five grams which is treated as a supply charge. It's serious. Today is sentencing. His lawyer points out that this school student has never been to court, did something youthful and stupid and the judge should exercise a good deal of leniency. Otherwise his client's hopes for a future career as a doctor might be squashed.

The police remind the judge of the scourge that is methamphetamine and the need to hold this young man accountable. A short term of imprisonment would do just that. By now his mother is weeping and the young man is swaying slightly in the dock. The baby is still jiggling on his mother's lap but is getting restless and making noises that are a distraction.

The judge is stern. He delivers a clear warning on the perils of selling drugs to friends. The young man thinks at this point he can hear the faint click of the prison door. But the judge steps back — metaphorically — to impose a community-based sentence.

The family quietly exhale.

Now that would have been the end of this true story, but the son's youthful stupidity knows no bounds.

That night, he goes on Facebook, declaring to his mates and anyone else in cyberspace how smart he was at putting one over the judge, how he acted all sorry when really he was thinking what a dick the judge was. And on it went. You get the drift.

A young woman happened to read the post. Her father was a judge, but not just any judge. She mentioned the post to him. 'Oh really,' he said. 'How interesting.'

The following day, he arranged for the young man and his lawyer to return to court.

Now at this point, you might wonder whether the judge had the power to reverse his decision. Indeed, he could and did.

In 1968 Chief Justice Wild set out three circumstances where a recall is possible. First, where the law has been amended; second, where a lawyer has failed to direct the court to legislation or a decision that is plainly relevant; and, third, where 'for some very special reason justice requires that the decision be recalled'.[34]

When people have never been to court before, it can be a daunting experience.

A youth hooning down the city's main street at 11.30 at

night, doing wheelies and yelling rude remarks at passers-by, is not thinking of the court. Nor does he think when dragging off another driver at the lights in his car. But when he sees twinkling lights behind him, he realises he has chosen the wrong car to drag off. It's the police, and a few months later he finds himself in court pleading guilty to a charge of sustained loss of traction. His car is impounded. He loses his licence for six months, so there goes the job together with his mates who need to find another car to hoon around in. On top of all that, he gets 100 hours' community work, which will keep him busy on a Saturday when he'd rather be lounging around drinking beer.

Next up is a middle-aged woman. She looks like the proverbial possum in the headlights, her face the same colour as dirty dishwater. It's significant that she is on her own because her erstwhile partner Harry is partly to blame for the predicament in which she finds herself.

Her name is called. She makes her way to the dock. Two security guards are also in the dock, making sure no one does a runner.

Everyone in the public gallery is staring at her wondering what she got nicked for.

It's benefit fraud. The amounts are read out as are all the dates of her offending when she claimed a benefit while living with Harry. Total owed: $123,562.78.

The lawyer for Work and Income notes that at $10 a week repayment, it will take the defendant 237 years to repay. Clearly not in her lifetime.

By now she is quietly weeping.

The judge is told that Harry had a tendency to come and go. He's an alcoholic and violent. He has never worked but expected her to put food on the table when he did turn up.

The circumstances sound a little like the case involving Isabella Ruka in 1997.[35] She omitted to tell the Department of Social Welfare that she was in a de facto relationship while claiming a benefit. She was convicted in both the

District Court and High Court. But in the Court of Appeal, the judges placed weight on Isabella's evidence that she felt trapped in the relationship by her partner's violence, lack of financial support for her and their child, and his relationship with other women. The Court of Appeal said the clear lack of financial support coupled with an absence of emotional commitment meant it was not 'a relationship in the nature of marriage', and the convictions were quashed.

As a result of that case, there are now criteria that Work and Income use to determine if a de facto relationship exists. One is sharing a dwelling whether full-time *or* part-time, which is where our weeping lady is caught. She and Harry have been living in the same house for 12 years. His absences follow a pattern in which he takes off every six months or so but is only away for days at a time.

A reparation order is put in place, despite the futility of it. She must also undertake 350 hours of community work, close to the maximum of 400. She leaves the court sad and angry at the same time. She's furious at Harry and vows to kick him out when she gets home.

The next sobbing female in the dock is only 19. She's a flight attendant who, as her lawyer tells the court, wants to work on international flights and fears a conviction for her first drink-driving offence will hinder her career. Well, in the post-Covid world, it's not clear what demand there will be for cabin staff. But the judge listens carefully to the facts. Two glasses of wine and no food were enough to put this slightly built young woman over the legal limit. To add insult to injury, she was acting as the sober driver for her friends who were considerably more inebriated than she was.

The lawyer argues for a discharge without conviction, which would preserve her clean record. Under section 107 of the Sentencing Act, the judge must not discharge an offender without conviction unless satisfied that the direct and indirect consequences of a conviction would be out of all proportion to the gravity of the offence.

Was it a one-off event?

Was the offending out of character?

The police are neutral, which is an endorsement of the discharge application. If she was sobbing at the start, she's heaving great gulps, tears and snot everywhere, overwhelmed with gratitude when the judge reaches the end of his lengthy decision to tell her she can go free.

All of the above examples are based on real cases with which I have dealt. I have yet to see a cocky defendant in the dock on their first charge. It's the ones who know the court like the back of their hand who display an attitude of insolence. Like the arrogant criminal going down a set of stairs. You call them a condescending con descending. And that, dear reader, is why I never told a joke in court.

18 In their ivory towers

I HAVE HEARD it said that judges are people who never live in the real world, that they attend private school, then head off to university before settling into a firm. Some go out on their own as barristers before going to the bench. All in all, it's a smooth ride, untroubled by poverty, unemployment or the myriad things ordinary New Zealanders struggle with from time to time.

Like academics in their ivory towers, we judges don't know what life's *really* like. An interesting notion, but certainly a far-fetched one.

It's apparent from my chapter on how it began that my background didn't include the usual scenario of leaving school and going to uni. There were a few twists and turns where money was tight and raising three lively children was challenging.

What I didn't dwell on in that story, though, was the particular anguish Mike and I lived through for 20 years. It coloured our lives and left us broken and, perhaps more than any other single event, shaped us as people. For all my years on the bench, I always had a particular affinity for those with addictions, because our daughter Polly was a drug addict.

She was the middle child of three, sandwiched between her brother 17 months' older and a daughter three years younger. Hers was a gentle birth and we doted on her as parents. She slept, fed and smiled all at the right times, a marked difference from her brother who suffered colic and was, unbeknown to us at the time, dairy intolerant.

We named her Anna. After her came another daughter, Katherine, lively, outgoing and quite different.

When the children were five, four and nine months we moved to Switzerland where the older two went to school and absorbed the language as easily as breathing.

On our return to New Zealand at Christmas 1984, Swiss German remained the language the older two shared. All three attended the same primary school. As I was then embarking on a law degree, I would ride to university on my Nifty Fifty scooter and aim to have classes that finished in time to be at home when they arrived.

One day we learned of a man trying to chat up children after school. I schooled them all in stranger danger. We read books together. *No More Secrets for Me* by Oralee Wachter,[36] on the theme of sexual abuse, was a favourite.

We were a family who gave proper names to body parts. It was penis and vagina. I remember one night with a group of older ladies attending a prayer meeting at our house. Our son sent his youngest sister to announce that 'Matthew has a sore penis'. I think it more likely he simply put her up to it.

One day Anna, then aged 11, rang asking if we could pick her up early from a friend's place. That was unusual, but nothing more was said. I do remember seeing her in her room lying on the bed, facing the wall, but she would not say what was wrong.

It wasn't until she went to high school and started self-harming and skipping school that we discovered the horror of what had happened. While at the friend's house, she had been raped. She wouldn't let us go to the police.

We started her with counselling, which wasn't very

effective. She was by now uncharacteristically angry and self-loathing. From the quiet child we knew, she'd become the teenager who was a stranger to us. She dabbled in drugs, then was introduced to hard drugs by her first boyfriend Tom. We tried everything.

By now my law career was taking off. I flirted briefly with the idea of home schooling her, but she wouldn't have a bar of it. She stayed at school long enough to do some School Certificate subjects, attaining 94 per cent in English. She was a gifted writer.

Over the next decade we were called to hospitals as she attempted suicide, had drug overdoses, or on one memorable occasion jumped six metres off the top of a building onto a concrete floor. It was only after she had been lying on the ground for hours that someone heard her, and firemen managed to extract her from the narrow space. Later one of them came to the hospital to see 'the miracle girl who survived that fall'.

Drug use led inevitably to prostitution, which for me was even worse than the drugs. We alternated between financially supporting her and trying tough love.

One day while she was staying with us, I came home unexpectedly and found her unresponsive and blue on the floor. A needle lay nearby and a spoon on the stove suggested she'd got drugs, despite our best efforts. We later learned someone had sent her drugs in the post, concealed in a toy.

The ambulance officers warned us she might not recover, but we had been through this so often, we looked resigned. They must have thought we were callous. Survive she did, but with some significant memory loss for a time. And so it was back to the drugs.

Mike had written a play, *Jerusalem, Jerusalem*, about the last year of poet James K. Baxter's life. It lay gathering dust in the bottom drawer until a friend read the script and persuaded him to have it performed. I assumed the role of director and we auditioned for the 13 actors needed.

Anna by this time had changed her name to Polly Anna Arabella Ruth Riddell — a mouthful I took some time to adjust to but, hey, a name change was the least of our worries.

She wanted to play the part of the young angry feminist who got to rage at Baxter. I sat her down and explained this project was important to her dad, that she couldn't miss a rehearsal or performance. If she made the commitment, she had to stick to it. She did, even when Tom, her first love, had a drug overdose and his life support was eventually switched off. Katherine took her to the beach after that, and they enacted a ceremony of letting Tom go. We wouldn't let her attend the funeral, fearful it would send her spiralling down again. But she faithfully played the role for the duration of the Dunedin season in October 2002, then was a cast member when we took the play to Christchurch and Wellington, early the following year.

It had been suggested to us we should take the play to the Edinburgh Fringe Festival, so we tested it in other New Zealand theatres. It was a great success.

We fundraised the necessary money to fly 15 people to the UK and pay them $200 per week. We put the play on to great crowds in the unheard-of Scottish heatwave of August 2003.

In the audience one night were a couple of young guys testing out their own brand of humour with their show. They gave us all free tickets and said come along. They were Flight of the Conchords.

By the time we did our last performance at an arts festival in Cheltenham, England we had performed our roles more than 39 times. We were starting to feel like Agatha Christie's *Mousetrap* for longevity.

On our return to New Zealand, Polly went on to train as a picture framer and, with an ACC payout, put a deposit on a wee house near the sea in Brighton, Dunedin. From 2003 that was her haven, and we developed the hope that maybe the tough years were behind her.

Then two months after I became a judge, we got a phone call. Polly had been in a head-on smash while texting. She had broken three vertebrae in her back, badly damaged her ankle, and had come within a whisper of being a tetraplegic. She came to stay with us, in a wheelchair for months, then walking slowly. By the end of the year the bones had largely healed, although pins held her ankle together and a steel rod remained in her back.

Then, that Christmas, Katherine found a needle in the bathroom, casually on display. She was furious, especially as her small son was running around. So, we packed Polly on a plane back to her house in Dunedin.

Life went on. By now she was on the methadone detoxification programme. As an articulate woman, she was a bit of a poster girl for the programme, someone who could live, work and function while on methadone.

Then evil broke in again.

Polly was raped while she was half asleep at a friend's house. But this time she went to the police. It turned out there were others, six victims of the same man. Polly persuaded them to go to the police as well.

The perpetrator pleaded guilty and got 13 years in prison. Polly wrote her own victim impact statement. In it she said in part:

'While X will be dealt by the court, I am sentenced to a lifetime of flashbacks, panic attacks, endless hours of counselling, mental instability — and lurking at the back of my head is that old black hound, depression. There is the possible potential for more self-harm and attempts at suicide. I don't mean to sound fatalistic or melodramatic. These are simply some of the dark truths that rarely see the light of day.

'There has been a domino effect of negative life choices on my part, which I need to both take responsibility for and learn to heal from. All of this stems from sexual abuse.

Writing this victim impact statement, and reflecting on it, I hope to take a step towards reclaiming my voice, my space, and beginning to heal and reclaim what was taken from me.

'I recall asking a friend when the legal process began, if I did bring about my own death/suicide, did she think more light might be shone on this case, and the general issue of rape culture in NZ. I'm relieved in hindsight that she said no, she thought that it would be a thousand times more powerful to survive this process, this awful journey and that in standing my ground and following it through, I wasn't letting him win.'

When Mike was diagnosed with prostate cancer, the thought of losing her beloved dad was unbearable. We holidayed in Central Otago early in 2018 and Polly came too. She seemed calmer, more at peace and was filling up journals faster than I could buy them for her.

When we decided to move to Central Otago, she was adamant she was coming too and the land next to the house we bought was intended to be Polly's Place.

On her fortieth birthday, Polly joined her brother in a trip to Switzerland. She had saved up for two years and we agreed to match her savings, dollar for dollar. They had a wonderful time exploring where we had lived, and she returned jubilant about the life ahead of her.

Five weeks later she was dead.

She'd visited a guy she'd had a relationship with, had some drugs and was unconscious for 14 hours before he thought to call an ambulance. Her phone calls to various family the night before convinced us this was no suicide. She had spoken enthusiastically about returning to the Ida Valley the following day.

In the short time she'd been staying in the valley, she endeared herself to farmers and writers alike. No one met Polly who didn't remember the encounter. Her purple hair and colourful clothes, her passionate convictions, her naive, childlike outlook was never squashed despite all that life threw at her.

I think she followed the mantra of Dr Seuss: why fit in when you can stand out?

At her funeral, I read out a poem Polly had written for my birthday earlier in the year. She had always managed to get lost travelling from Brighton to Central Otago, and the poem, titled 'Follow the Signs', encompassed that and her gratitude to us both as parents.

> The first time
> I drove to Oturehua
> Dad said,
> Just follow the signs.
> Yet still
> I got lost.
> I've always had
> A hopeless sense
> Of direction
> And of time.
> And so,
> I've anchored
> My trust
> When it comes
> To these two things
> So often
> In the both
> Of you.
> For a long, long time
> There's been something
> Weighty
> Within me.
> Once a crow's nest
> Woven from number eight wire
> Eight, the number of chaos,

Ate, for the years
Eaten away.
Now, in its place
A turning, spitting, churning, ticking
Burning fire
Within.
Into which I throw
The old things
I have no need for.
The weight of
Bitterness.
The stones, the unknown,
The ungrown,
And of the known too.
In its place takes
A calm notion of things.
Solid
Ground beneath my
Steel capped boots.
In its place the
Glimpse of a path
way
I'll call my own.
The weight and wait
By night, by day,
Grow lighter.
And although my body, mind
And soul may have been badly
Broken
I love to sit and watch
Rainbows
Reflecting on the walls
Which would not be there,
Were there no cracks
To let the light in.
Nor were it for the rain

As the Gods weep gently
With joy.
The second time I left Oturehua
Dad winked
And said
'Don't forget to follow the signs.'
But I didn't get lost,
Haven't since,
For the signs grow brighter,
Clearer
As each day goes
By.
Splashing rainbows,
Breadcrumbs
Leading me
Back
All the way
Home.

We hoped for a calm, safe existence for Polly living next to us. That wasn't to be.

And why have I related this story of Polly?

Because we judges aren't spared pain and loss. Like everyone else, we see the anguish of living. I know, from my relationship with fellow judges, that they have struggles with all kinds of gut-wrenching sadness. The woman in the Family Court who said to me, 'Judge, you don't know what it's like' didn't need me to correct her, but she was wrong, and I wanted to tell her about my Polly.

Nor have we judges cornered the market on successful parenting. Certainly, there are those whose children go to Oxford or Cambridge and have stellar careers. But there are others.

In our case, success at one time meant she was doing well on methadone or completing a drug rehab programme, but that's not the kind of success you necessarily want to share. Except that, early on, I decided I wouldn't hide Polly away. I was proud of who she was, even if she didn't fit the usual definition of success.

I talked about her to groups, to mothers, to lawyers.

In my last bar dinner held for me by the local Law Society when I retired, I spoke of Polly. I know such an occasion is a time to tell a few well-placed jokes, then sit down. But Polly had died only five weeks before and my sense of humour had deserted me.

I spoke of pain and loss, of a vibrant daughter, of the struggles we all have and of how tough this job can be, for lawyers, judges, court staff, everyone. I concluded by saying that the best we can hope for is to love and be loved by our children.

Afterwards, a steady stream of people came up to me to tell me of their particular loss, a brother who had committed suicide, a mother who died recently, of sexual abuse, of unexpected death. People from whom I least expected such sorrow.

I read somewhere that it is said, grief does not change you. It reveals you. Mike and I had always felt a bit broken as we struggled to live with Polly's addiction. Her death hollowed us out in new ways.

Often, I have grieved the things I didn't do or should have done for Polly. One day in the middle of such a spiel, Katherine said in a moment of great insight, 'Mum, you take too much credit for our failures.'

19 My learned friend

THERE HAS TO BE a chapter about lawyers. It wouldn't be complete without their contribution. Nor would it be fair to write about lawyers without adding at least one lawyer joke. So here it is.

A number of wealthy couples were enjoying an afternoon on a friend's 60-foot luxury schooner. The wine flowed freely and the canapés were circulated. With the gentle rock of the boat, they became a little inebriated and unsteady on their feet. One of their number, a lawyer, fell overboard. Horrified, the rest watched as sharks quickly circled the man, then inexplicably all swam away.

Those on board were amazed. Not his wife. 'Professional courtesy,' she said.

Lawyers, by and large, do a fine job for their clients, putting their case at sentencing, representing them at trial and, of course, providing legal advice outside the courtroom. It's not an easy job. People instruct a lawyer because something has gone wrong and they want the lawyer to fix it and fast. But the courts are part of the Ministry of Justice, a cumbersome monolith which moves at a glacial pace and may seem, to the uninitiated, designed to impede the flow of justice rather than facilitate it. They blame their lawyers for delays, lawyers blame the courts, the public blame the judges, talkback radio blames everyone. It's a roller-coaster.

Let's remember, though, that many lawyers never see the inside of a courtroom. Theirs is a life of corporate takeovers, insurance and insolvencies. I remember the story of a lawyer who envisaged a life of litigation for himself, standing up for the little guy and taking up the cudgel on behalf of those who had no voice. The first time he appeared in court on a minor matter, he was so terrified by the ferocity of the judge and the whole courtroom palaver that he left, never to return. He spent his days thereafter doing conveyancing.

It can be challenging, especially for a young lawyer in court. I have watched as they read from a prepared sheet, 'May it please Your Honour, counsel's name is . . .' Even their own name is written in full, fearful they may forget that too. Being in the same courtroom for a number of years is a great opportunity for a judge to observe a new lawyer develop confidence and legal skills. In some cases, those same lawyers go to the bar, not your local, but a term used to denote those who strike out on their own as barristers. They are distinguished from solicitors who work in a firm or practice on their own but operate a trust account, unlike barristers.

To continue the alcohol analogy, those who are barristers practise at what is known as the independent bar.

The distinction between barristers and solicitors is little understood in New Zealand and is not as noteworthy as across the ditch. In Australia, only barristers generally go to court. The solicitor may meet with the client and prepare the court documents but will then hand them over to a barrister.

My friend who practised law in Australia for many years recalls announcing himself in court one day. He was a solicitor from the Gold Coast. The judge learned of this and flung a law book off the bench in disgust.

In England, the distinction matters a great deal. Barristers wear wig and gown. Solicitors do not. Barristers work on the more complex cases and are paid more, but do not have the benefit of sick pay or maternity leave, unlike their solicitor colleagues.

There is an idiosyncratic practice in England where barristers do not shake hands. It's nothing to do with Covid. Indeed, the custom predates the pandemic by centuries, back to a time where a handshake demonstrated to another that you were not armed. 'By gripping each other by the right hand, you were showing them that your hand wasn't on the hilt of your sword.'[37] Since barristers were gentlemen, they trusted each other implicitly and therefore there was no need to shake hands.

It is mainly barristers who are appointed as judges in the UK. Not so in New Zealand, where the judiciary is drawn from the ranks of both barristers and solicitors.

Any lawyer may apply to become a Queen's Counsel or QC. It is an appointment reserved for senior practitioners and is usually granted to barristers. The influence of English life lingers on here as becoming a QC is known as 'taking silk' or 'being called to the inner bar'. They are both English terms that probably mean little to the average Kiwi.

Throughout this book, I have used the generic term 'lawyer', which is instantly recognisable. Lawyers in court refer to each other as 'my learned friend', a term which can also be mystifying to the average punter who may wonder why they need to remind each other of their buddy status. There are other possibilities. They could be 'my amigo', or 'my confrère' or even 'my chum'. But no. It's 'my learned friend', even when things are decidedly frosty between them.

I started out as a lawyer later than most. I was 40 when admitted to the bar as a barrister and solicitor and was grateful to the firm who gave me a start. I was with them for five years, becoming an associate before our decision to live at the other end of the country.

The thing about being a newly minted lawyer is the judge can usually gauge by your age that you haven't lived long enough to complete any more than high school and law school, so they cut you some slack. Not so for a

40-year-old. And that is where my learned friend helped or hindered my fledgling career.

I remember being sent to court one day by my supervising partner to put in a brief appearance for my client, but I was also told to do my best to get the whole thing thrown out. I didn't know if he was serious, but with semi-youthful enthusiasm, I thought I would give it a go.

At the appointed time, I rose to my feet, went through the motions and then bravely asked for a strike-out application. The judge enquired which part of the District Court Rules I was relying on. Good question, to which I had no ready answer. I asked for a brief adjournment, which was granted. I looked around frantically. My learned friend was sitting nearby, and he had the Rules in front of him. He was happy to point me in the right direction and later I went back to the office to proudly report the outcome. More senior lawyers can be real friends when you're new to the legal world.

Others, I must say, were less helpful. In the cut and thrust of the Auckland law scene, I found a rather brutal, even feral attitude between lawyers, which made the later move to Dunedin even more of a revelation. There, law was the preserve of the polite and affable. It was such that I was surprised to be concluding a conveyancing transaction one Friday afternoon and went to the lawyer's office to be offered a wee dram, to seal the deal as it were.

Notwithstanding that story, law is a demanding profession and not for the faint-hearted. Once you are armed with your law degree and have a few years' experience under your belt, though, you will be au fait not only with the depth of meaning in 'my learned friend', but also all the other cryptic sayings in the court, especially those voiced by the judge, like:

'You are pushing against an open door.' In other words, you've won your argument; you don't need to make the point further.

'I can't hear you' doesn't mean your voice hasn't carried.

But it could be you are not entitled to speak.

There are those judges who want to cut off the lawyer at the knees. One of our number, who has since died, was, in practice and on the bench, quick with a retort. While he was a lawyer, on one occasion he was counsel for the appellant, a man who was seeking to appeal a decision of the District Court. The judge, large in stature and girth, kept interrupting, talking over him, cutting him off. At one point, the judge leaned back in his chair and said, 'I think I can see the picture you are trying to paint,' and quick as a flash our lawyer replied, 'Well, it would help if you didn't keep moving the easel so much.'

Just remember, when lawyers preface their submissions to the judge with increasingly fawning 'with great respect' or 'with the greatest respect' and that beauty, 'with the greatest possible respect', you know these are all tantamount to 'I don't exactly hate you, but if you were on fire and I had water, I'd drink it.'

20 Writing decisions

AT THE CONCLUSION of a judge-alone trial or in Family Court proceedings, it is the judge's job to make a decision and, in doing so, to set out the reasons for that decision.

It should be apparent to the parties reading it why the judge has reached a particular conclusion, taking the law and the facts into account.

It is not an easy task. I have laboured over some decisions for far longer than was probably necessary. I do not agree with the saying that any decision is better than no decision. Which reminds me of the old joke about the psychiatrist who asks his patient if she has trouble making decisions. And the patient says, 'Well, doctor, yes and no.'

There is an art to writing decisions. Through their judicial career, judges attend seminars to help them refine their judgments, leave out the superfluous, use plain language, and write in a more precise and compelling way.

It is not enough for a judge to recall the facts and say why they have found for the defendant or applicant. The facts of the case are, of course, important. They are the reason why we are here. But any fact scenario is likely to have occurred before and been the subject of deliberation by a judge.

In this way, case law has developed, which is simply a record of other decisions.

Take, for example, an assault. A person charged with such an offence is dealt with under section 194 of the Crimes Act, which states the maximum penalty is two years' prison for an assault on a child under 14 years or by a male on a female. There have been, sadly, many cases under this section, each evolving the definition of assault. Some decisions have been appealed to higher courts, leading to more refined interpretations and more precise guidelines for judges who come to sentence a person convicted of such a charge.

Consequently, it's important to read case law to take account of how other judges have treated similar fact scenarios, particularly in the High Court and Court of Appeal.

Let me give another example.

A child has been arbitrarily removed from, say, Napier, where she lived with her mother, visiting Dad fortnightly. Suddenly she's in Dunedin with Mum and the new boyfriend. An urgent hearing is heard to determine if, in the interim, the child must be returned to Napier until the substantive (or main) hearing occurs.

A judge isn't left to wonder whether the cities of Napier or Dunedin are more beneficial for the child. The High Court already dealt with a similar scenario[38] and concluded that, unless there are compelling reasons, the status quo should prevail — for now.

In other words, Napier is the winner. Any judge deciding a snatch and run case like this is likely to refer to that High Court case as authority for the proposition 'return the child'. If, on the other hand, there has been family violence and Mum flees to a town where she has good family support, the outcome might be different.

I have at times written two decisions on a case in the Family Court.

The first is for the parents. It follows the facts and law scenario set out above. Then I write a much shorter decision. That one is for the child. Written in language a child can understand, it sets out what I have decided to do and why. You could call it a letter.

When a child is drawn into the conflict between parents, knows the push and pull of the tussle involving them, has their own lawyer, and comes to court to meet the judge, I figure they are due the respect of a response from the judge, even if they are only eight years old.

There are notable fine examples of decision making, particularly in the United Kingdom and United States.

Lord Denning was a judge who died at the age of 100 after a 38-year career handing down what were often seen as simple decisions that overrode the precedent that had gone before.

In that sense he was a judicial activist, shaping the law according to the times, rather than relying on the way it had always been. As such, he was criticised for remaking the law.

But he knew how to begin a judgment.

In one, he wrote: 'The defendant has in the past occasionally had a wager on a horse race. Today she has been taking part in another game of chance or skill — the game of litigation.'[39]

In another case, he noted, 'This case ought to have been simple, but the lawyers have made it complicated.'[40]

And one more: 'This case concerns an accident which took place in the sausage department of the defendant's food factory in Cadby Hall.' That one is worth quoting further. 'At 2.30 in the afternoon the tea break was called. The plaintiff, a married woman, was the first off towards the tea bar. She was always, the judge said, pretty quick off the mark for her cup of tea.'[41]

American judges are known for attempting to jolly up their decisions with a spot of poetry:

'Twas the night before Christmas, when all through the jail, not an inmate was stirring, they couldn't make bail.'[42]

Even the Court of Appeals in Georgia has been known to have a go, starting a decision with:

'The DA was ready
His case was red hot.
Defendant was present,
His witness was not.'

Or this effort from a dissenting judge in 2002 concerning a prenuptial agreement:

'A groom must expect matrimonial pandemonium
when his spouse finds he's given her a cubic zirconium
instead of a diamond in her engagement band,
the one he said was worth twenty-one grand.'[43]

Enough of this doggerel, which a New Zealand judge would never stoop to, though some have started their decisions with a certain degree of pithiness. It was the late Justice Hammond who began a 1993 Appeal decision, about an owner who had failed to register his dog, with the words: 'There is in Auckland, a handsome German shepherd called Ben.'

His decision concluded: '*Cave canem* (for the uninitiated, beware of the dog)'.[44]

I think my favourite for its demonstration of flair and irony came from an Australian High Court judge. He was deciding a case where the deceased was survived by one lawful and two de facto wives. He began:

'The deceased appears to have maintained simultaneous domestic establishments with all three women and their respective children. In terms of division of his time, he appears to have given preference to Margaret Green, but it seems that he spent two nights a week, regularly, with the respondent and gave what she regarded as a plausible explanation for his absences. Presumably, over a number of years, he managed to achieve the same result with the other women. This is consistent with his apparent success as a used car salesman.'[45]

The trick is to walk the fine line between being succinct and simply naff. Law is too serious a business and too much hangs on a decision to engage in idle whimsy.

Writing a reserved decision means a judge has time to reflect on matters: the tone and language for starters. When a decision is delivered at the conclusion of the trial or hearing, it's known as an oral decision. Try as we might to be measured and mindful, the tongue can get away on us, as I found once.

I had heard an application in the Family Court for a separation order, a relatively rare creature, since these days if a party believes the relationship is over, they simply move out.

In this case the parties were recent African immigrants. The wife wanted a separation order, which was vehemently opposed by the husband.

In my decision, granting the order, I went to some lengths to explain to the man that New Zealand has culturally different expectations than where he was from. I went on to say that women are allowed to be independent, forge their own path after a relationship ends and could have 20 relationships if she wished.

He looked even more worried than at the start of the hearing.

Maybe I was overstating my case and setting up his now ex-wife for allegations of immoral behaviour. But I was by now part-way through the decision. There was no turning back.

A good decision must first traverse the facts of the case. Then the judge must set out the opposing arguments, so it's clear they have considered them. Next, it's on to the law, with a summation of other similar cases, before some discussion of the various merits and a conclusion that, by the end, should state the obvious outcome fortified by law and facts.

Occasionally the judge will conclude with an observation about the case, and perhaps express the hope that these parties can now move on, as I have often expressed in hearings involving warring adults.

Sometimes I have wanted to end with a little pithy saying like, 'Marriage is like a deck of cards: in the beginning all you need is two hearts and a diamond; by the end, you wish you had a club and a spade.'

But I never did.

21 Justice must be seen to be done

A CALVIN AND HOBBES cartoon has Dad intoning, 'The world isn't fair, Calvin.' Calvin replies, 'I know, Dad, but why isn't it ever unfair in my favour?' Fairness is a word that besets children and adults alike.

When I was growing up, we had a family rule. When it came to cutting the cake, 'You cut, I choose'. Whichever way you cut, it had to be fair.

Fairness was the maxim which underpinned most things and it set the standard for me in later life. I have always felt a sense of outrage when things were not fair.

Later, as a lawyer and then judge, I felt it wasn't enough for justice to be done — it must be seen to be done as well. If I thought that was original, I was wrong. In fact, the phrase and the meaning of it date back to an English case in 1924.

A Mr McCarthy was charged with dangerous driving on his motorcycle. The judge's clerk belonged to a firm of solicitors who had sued Mr McCarthy in a civil claim relating to the accident. The judges duly convicted Mr McCarthy, without conferring with the clerk it must be said.

When Mr McCarthy appealed, the Lord Chief Justice Hewart held that, while there had been no question of inappropriate interference by the clerk in the decision-making process, his mere presence was enough to taint the case with bias.

The decision was famous for holding that not only must justice be done, it must also be seen to be done. Mr McCarthy's conviction was quashed.[46]

Ironically, the Lord Chief Justice was not known for his impartiality at the time, but with this decision he hit the nail on the head and, nearly a century later, his famous phrase is an integral part of judicial life.

So how does the judicial system impart not only justice but also the appearance of justice?

First, people must have ample notice that they are required to answer a charge.

That principle is sometimes overridden in the Family Court where in cases of family violence or those of similar urgency, a party can apply on an urgent basis for an order, without reference to the other side.

There a judge can make a decision, such as a Protection Order, which is then communicated to the other side, who can choose to defend it. Such applications, also known as *ex parte* (in the interests of one side only), weigh up the importance of advance notice and deem personal safety to take priority.

Aside from cases of urgency where an interim decision must override the need for adequate notice, the principle remains vitally important. People must have time to respond to a charge, so that they can prepare their defence.

The second principle is that a person has a fair hearing.

Where the police bring a charge, it is up to them to prove the elements of a crime. If the defendant chooses to remain silent, they have that right. It is not for the defendant to prove innocence. A fair hearing means the court should hear all the evidence and a defendant should have access to a lawyer or have specifically declined that opportunity.

The third principle is that there is no bias involved.

Mr McCarthy's case is a good example. In New Zealand, if a judge knows one of the witnesses, for instance, that judge must recuse themself, to avoid any perception of bias, even if no actual bias exists.

It is imperative that a person has a fair hearing, free from any taint of partiality.

My husband Mike in his misspent youth travelled to Morocco and, with friends, smoked large quantities of hash provided in an isolated setting in the mountains.

After purchasing more, they were caught eventually at roadblocks designed to fleece dopey foreigners. Smoking hash was legal at the time in Morocco, so they were charged with tobacco grown without a permit.

They nominated one of their number to represent them in court. The charge was read. He stood. 'Your Honour.'

'*Suffi*,' said the judge, a shortened version of the French *suffisant* which he probably used often. Enough! And sentence was pronounced. Four months' prison.

What made it more galling was that the electric razor and watch Mike used to purchase the hashish sat prominently on the Chief of Police's desk after they were arrested.

We take it for granted in New Zealand that everyone will be afforded a fair trial, not as the Queen in *Alice of Wonderland* would have it. 'No, no. Sentence first, verdict afterwards.'

We all want a fair suck of the kūmara and to have it make sense.

Giving reasons for a decision is said to be part of the process of open justice. It helps the parties understand how the judge has regarded their arguments.

It accords with judicial accountability and it provides future cases with an indication of how those matters have been dealt with in the past.

Sometimes a matter doesn't get as far as a trial.

On one memorable day in court, I threw out three different cases after each had been remanded many times without seemingly any progress. I'm sure the lawyers in court thought they were on a roll, as each stood offering stories of delay, lack of disclosure of the case by police or, in one case the defendant had to repeatedly take time off work for court appearances and had already been to court six times.

The headlines read: 'Judge dismisses long-delayed prosecutions'.

The police were not happy and were quoted as saying, 'It's not a good look.' But witnesses' memories fade, defendants can be subject to bail conditions that become onerous and, in the end, as I said at the time, it's a breach of natural justice. The wheels of justice grind slowly enough without unreasonable delays being added to the mix.

Justice must be heard as well as seen.

The courts have loop systems for the hard of hearing and, occasionally, deaf interpreters are brought in to assist parties when that is requested.

One of my colleagues recalled her first mediation conference in the Family Court with an elderly couple.

The wife spoke, for a long time. When it was the husband's turn, he said he hadn't put batteries in his hearing aid and couldn't hear anything — which gave added meaning to the wife's lament that you never listen to me anyway.

Another aspect which people sometimes find hard to see as justice is the issue of name suppression, particularly where the defendant might be a public figure. The court may suppress a person's name where extreme hardship is likely to occur to the defendant or family.

Being well known isn't sufficient. Nor is the shame of having one's name splashed all over the media enough.

The bar is set very high before the court will grant name suppression. That is because the principle of open justice is important. To overrule that principle requires something like a real risk of prejudice to a fair trial or a certain hardship to the victim.

The far-reaching nature of Facebook and Twitter has sometimes made a mockery of Suppression Orders, as we have seen in recent times. While a name might be supressed in New Zealand, there is easy access to it through overseas social media. The global village of which we are a part can then render such orders ineffectual.

Interestingly, the numbers of Suppression Orders are decreasing each year, from over 2000 in 2010 to under 1400 in 2019.

If justice is to be seen to be done, perhaps there is less place in our society for these orders, particularly in the age of multiple internet platforms.

Adequate notice of any hearing, a fair hearing and the lack of any bias are the three platforms on which our justice system rests. We may not get it right all the time, but we must tirelessly pursue them as our goals.

It has been said that justice is blind until a judge gives it eyes. The blindfold is a symbolic image depicted on the statue of Lady Justice. She wears one to denote she is blind to a person's race or creed, wealth or poverty. She carries the scales, indicating the balancing exercise involved in decision making. In her other hand is the sword of judicial power. Other commentators attribute the sword to its ability to cut through conflicting evidence to the core of truth, which sounds to me a tad less militaristic and more about discernment.

In countries such as the United States, Lady Justice is curiously depicted without her blindfold, perhaps a worrying development.

Finally, of course, after the hearing there is the decision issued after due consideration of all the facts.

If justice is to be seen to be done, as Socrates put it, a judge must hear courteously, answer wisely, consider soberly and decide impartially. Sombre words from two and a half thousand years ago.

22 It's all Parliament's fault

LAWS IN NEW ZEALAND begin life as a bill. They go through several stages, from their introduction to Parliament, to first, second and third readings in the House, to approval and the Royal assent by the Governor-General.

Usually it is the government that introduces a bill, but sometimes the subject matter of a bill is drawn out of the hat as it were, by ballot. Other times a Member of Parliament introduces what is known as a private bill or local bill.

Back in 1979, New Zealand was said to make the fastest law in the west. A huge number of bills were introduced and rushed through at a pace that was regarded as constitutionally questionable. The mixed-member proportional (MMP) system introduced after 1993 means more constraint because generally the government of the day needs the support of another party to pass a law.

During the passage of a bill, it is advertised so the public can respond with submissions in favour or against. Six weeks is the usual timeframe. Any less and there are likely to be cries of democracy denied.

All in all, it is a lengthy process designed to weed out errors and contradictions, so that the final law is clear in its terms and free of ambiguity. That's the idea. But, as we know, life's not like that, and it's the judges who must deal with laws that are obsolete or just plain wrong. I'm going to give you some examples.

Let's begin with the worst illustration. The Adoption Act was passed in 1955. That should give you a clue. No statute on the books is free from fustiness and irrelevance after all that time and the Adoption Act is no exception.

The act was passed at a time when families were very different. Same-sex relationships, surrogacy, unmarried couples were all unheard of (or at least were underground). And the idea that a child had legal rights hadn't entered the public consciousness. Applying the Adoption Act to those scenarios has therefore required some stretching of the law. Section 3 allows 'two spouses' to apply to adopt a child. Courts have now held that spouses may be an unmarried couple or a couple who have separated but not divorced. Probably not what Parliament had in mind back in 1955.

But it's worse than that. Some decisions have declared the act to be inconsistent with the New Zealand Bill of Rights as well as our obligations under the United Nations Convention on the Rights of the Child.

For Māori, it has been a disaster. Section 19 states that no one shall adopt a child in accordance with Māori custom. Prior to that, Māori adoption, whāngai, had legal status. Whāngai meant there was no secrecy, children knew their birth parents and maintained contact with them. The children knew their whakapapa, or genealogy, and whānau, hapū and iwi could take part in making whāngai decisions. All that was wiped out by the Adoption Act.

There's a very personal cost, described in eloquent terms in the book *Tree of Strangers*[47] by New Zealand author Barbara Sumner, who was adopted 10 days after her birth. She writes from the perspective of the adopted person. 'No one sought our consent to be removed from our mothers, heritage and cultures. Most of us lost our identity without any legal representation. There is no mechanism to reclaim our original identity.'[48]

The Adoption Act focuses on the people adopting a child and the process involved. It gives little thought to the child, but, Sumner writes, '[w]e often hear that a mother *gave away* her baby. People are not objects. You cannot *give* us away. These terms ignore the fundamental human rights of the mother and her child. Every mother of loss I've spoken to experienced coercion and pressure to sign away their right to parent. Some of us see that as abduction.'

The Adoption Act should not be tinkered with or amended further. It needs to be replaced.

The next example was born out of a cry for harsher penalties in the belief that would reduce crime. As I have said earlier in this book, such a proposed policy was good for attracting votes at election time. I'm referring to what is known as New Zealand's current three strikes policy. The best way to describe why this legislation is a failure is to give you an example of it in action.

Daniel Fitzgerald had his challenges, being a schizophrenic who suffered head injuries which left him mentally impaired, and with a history of drug and alcohol abuse. He had consistently been on medication, with varying success. In 2012 he was convicted of indecent assault and again in 2015. He received 11 months in prison for the first offence and four months for the second. Both offences were more serious than what happened next in 2016 when he went up to two women in Cuba Street, Wellington, told one of them he wanted to kiss her and tried to. She moved her face, but he managed to kiss her on the cheek.

The other woman tried to pull him away. He grabbed her arms, pushed her against a nearby wall and held her there for a moment, then let go and kept walking.

The court acknowledged it was a distressing incident for both women. It must also be said it was a brief encounter, lasting one to two minutes.

Mr Fitzgerald was arrested and charged with indecent assault of the first woman, common assault of the second and breach of an extended Supervision Order because he had consumed alcohol. He was found guilty at trial. On the assault charge he was convicted and given three months' prison. He was convicted but received no penalty for the breach of the Supervision Order.

The indecent assault charge, an attempted kiss on the lips and actual kiss on the cheek, involved, as the court said, 'conduct at the low end of the range for that offence' and 'it would not normally attract a jail term'.

But Mr Fitzgerald had two previous indecent assault convictions which were caught by the three strikes law. So, under section 86D (2) of the Sentencing Act this was his third conviction, albeit a minor one and the maximum sentence would apply. That was seven years' prison. And the judge would have no discretion. The judge would have to impose a sentence that bore no relationship at all to the gravity of the offending or to the circumstances of the offender.

Mr Fitzgerald sought a discharge without conviction under section 106 of the Sentencing Act as the only way to avoid the seven years. That wasn't granted because the exception in section 106 (1) said '. . . unless by any enactment applicable to the offence the court is required to impose the minimum sentence'. And the three strikes law required the court to impose the minimum, that is, seven years.

In the Court of Appeal,[49] the judges agreed that section 106 could not apply to Mr Fitzgerald who had been sentenced to seven years' prison in the lower court. They also found that the three strikes law in section 86D (2) could produce results that were inconsistent with our Bill of Rights Act. The fact that other results may be unobjectionable doesn't save it.

Mr Fitzgerald is still in prison.

The next example has vexed judges and I know because I have had to consider it since the change to the law was passed in 2017. Section 18A of the Oranga Tamariki Act allows Oranga Tamariki, the Ministry for Children, to immediately remove a child at birth from the mother if, in the past, that mother has had a child taken from her by the ministry.

The rationale for this amendment to the act was to set a standard, so if the mother had been deemed unable to care for a child before, Oranga Tamariki could step in swiftly before the mother's inability to parent became obvious again.

That sounds well and good.

But people change, learn new skills and years later may be quite a different parent from the 16-year-old whose boyfriend was physically abusive to the baby. Even if a mother doesn't develop good parenting practices, the removal of a Māori child to, say, a Pākehā family is in breach not only of the Oranga Tamariki Act but also our obligations under the United Nations Declaration on the Rights of Indigenous Peoples, not to mention the UN's Convention on the Rights of the Child.

The Oranga Tamariki Act proclaims a commitment to the principles of the Treaty of Waitangi and to protecting a child's cultural identity. That is difficult if the child is removed to another part of the country to a family who don't know, let alone have any commitment to, the child's whakapapa.

Section 18A hearings to determine the right to uplift the newborn child are fraught, and there is often a distinct lack of evidence to support the uplift.

Jean Te Huia has been a midwife for 28 years. When she experienced a baby being removed moments after an emergency Caesarean delivery, she was told the mother was not allowed to see the baby as it was earmarked for foster care by Oranga Tamariki and would be picked up by its new foster parents later that day. As she said, 'This was the first either of us [she and the mother] had heard about this; we hadn't been involved in any conversations . . . That's when I realised I couldn't be part of a system that removed newborns from their mothers like that. Now it's my mission to make sure Māori women are safe from this insidious, unjust behaviour.'[50]

Further in that article, iwi leaders and Family Court lawyers say the practice of uplifting newborns hours after birth is creating a 'stolen generation' of Māori children, with a system so stacked against parents that regaining custody is almost impossible.

The final example is found in the Sentencing Act. The sentiment which gave rise to section 24A is, in my view, spot on. It is a more recent addition passed in 2014 which allows for a restorative justice conference to occur once a person has pleaded guilty, but before sentencing. Before 2014, judges had a discretion to refer eligible cases to such a conference. After 2014, it became mandatory. But is it?

Provision is made for such a conference 'in certain cases'. The section goes on to say if:

1. an offender appears for sentencing and
2. the offender has pleaded guilty and
3. there are one or more victims and
4. no restorative justice conference has previously occurred and
5. the Registrar has informed the court such a conference can be accessed
6. then the court *must* adjourn the proceedings to make enquiries about whether a conference is appropriate.

That sounds as mandatory as you can get. But unless there are restorative justice conveners in every court (and there aren't), judges find it easy to skim over section 24A and move straight to sentencing on the basis that number 5 above hasn't been met.

Our court system focuses on the punitive. That is, punish the offender. It usually does not look at restoration, how to put things right for *both* parties, the offender and the victim. Restorative justice is a concept which could revolutionise the justice system if fully applied. But it needs well-resourced representatives of the process in every court, so they can ensure the judge, lawyers and registrars all adhere to the implementation of section 24A.

Oh, if we had English prison and social reformer Elizabeth Fry's take on punishment. She said it is not for revenge, but to lessen crime and reform the criminal.

23 The vexatious litigant

OKAY, LET'S GET the definition out of the way first. A vexatious litigant is someone who brings a legal action solely intended to harass another party in circumstances where the action is without merit. They do it over and over again, until the court says, 'Enough!' and restricts their ability to bring any more proceedings for a certain period of time.

In England, such people are known colloquially as vexies.

Someone can be deemed vexatious without a limit put on future claims.

The Family Court has seen its fair share of vexatious litigants, inevitably self-represented and with a bone to pick with government departments. Police, Oranga Tamariki, Work and Income and the Attorney-General have all borne the brunt of the vexatious litigant. They are also recipients of the long, ranting letter, threatening legal proceedings, one million dollars in damages and demanding a public apology.

The sad thing is they may have started with a genuine grievance, then in time all sense of proportion is lost. Their days become a ceaseless round of drafting court documents and letters. They arrive at court with a bulging briefcase and a determined gleam in their eye. The judge shudders inside, knowing that what lies ahead could not, by any stretch of the imagination, be construed as reasonable.

Let me give you a real-life example from the High Court in 2017.[51] Mr O'Neill was the plaintiff. He wanted to recall a decision on an ACC matter in which the judge declined to grant him leave to appeal.

Mr O'Neill named the judge and two deputy registrars of the Auckland High Court as defendants. He claimed the judge was 'not a fit and proper person to hold judicial warrant, is a criminal and a pervert, not mentally competent to sit on judicial matters'. The registrars were said to have conspired against him, withheld evidence and generally been quite mean, that last description my interpretation of the legal terminology.

The judge examined the issues involved and whether Mr O'Neill's proceedings were frivolous or vexatious, or an abuse of process.

The answer? Yes, yes and yes.

To call any judge mentally incompetent, a criminal and a pervert is not only unwise but displays a breathtaking degree of ignorance. Certainly, it is not the way to win your case. But the vexatious litigant is blind to all this; they have lost all sense of proportion.

The same might be said of the Perth businessman Clive Palmer, who as the joke goes has more active legal proceedings on the go than there are recorded cases of Covid-19 in Western Australia. The *Sydney Morning Herald* discussed whether he could be declared a vexatious litigant, especially given that Mr Palmer once proclaimed litigation as his hobby.[52]

Vexatious litigants sometimes assume more imposing names, thinking that will lend weight to their case. So, in England, two gentlemen, Mr Hayward and Mr O'Neill (the latter is not our friend from the High Court above) have taken on the names of the previous Attorney-General and the Lord Chancellor to aid their petition.

The British Lord Chief Justice Thomas Bingham observed that the vexatious litigant continues when 'on any rational and objective assessment the time has come to stop'.[53]

Stop they do not. It brings heartache to other parties when, as happens in our Family Court, one party is hell-bent on litigating everything from access to guardianship matters (such as food choices for the children, immunisation and name changes).

Of course, there are those with a genuine claim. They are distinguished by their willingness to engage in mediation, inside or outside the court. But we're talking here about those who want to annoy the other parent, make them jump through hoops, waste their time and stall when resolution seems likely.

The Family Court can, at the end of a case, direct a vexatious litigant to refrain from bringing any more applications to the court for a period, without the court's permission. I have used that on occasion to debar a father from filing any fresh applications for two years.

Sometimes the vexatious litigant will take delight in cross-examining the mother in court. That step has been slowed in its tracks by section 95 of the Evidence Act which prevents such cross-examination where there has been domestic violence in the relationship. In that event, the court must appoint a lawyer to ask questions on behalf of the vexatious litigant. This avoids the potentially abusive situation where a woman who has been on the receiving end of family violence by her ex-partner has to sit through snide and demeaning questions by the abuser.

When I was first a lawyer, that provision did not apply and I remember one particularly brutish cross-examination of my female client, couched in terms that did not warrant legal objection but nevertheless subjected her to reliving the whole ghastliness of her abusive marriage.

It must be said the law catches on eventually, but slowly, slowly.

Ironically, in the Family Court vexatious litigants reveal themselves in more ways than they intend. For example, the father who insists on cold showers every winter's morning for the children or excessive exercise and holds forth on the parental failings of the mother is revealing much about himself. It sometimes leads to the question: well, has he the insight and compassion to do the best by his children, or is he so driven and oblivious to their needs that maybe the children should live exclusively with their mother?

If that decision is reached, and it's a painful one for the judge, all hell breaks loose. The judge might be stalked, followed home, or be subjected to vicious abuse on social media. The list goes on and they are all real examples. One of the worst in my view was the vexatious litigant who plastered the words 'Judge X is a rapist' all over the sides of his own van. And you can guess he didn't leave the vehicle in the garage.

We live in a democracy. People have the right to disagree, even strongly. We are all different. We're shaped by our upbringing, teachers and relationships. Someone who got the short end of the stick on any, or all, of those influences may have a very skewed view of life.

As a judge, I have endeavoured to be polite to vexatious litigants. As crazy as they might get, they are entitled to respect in the courtroom, like everyone else.

That can be challenging, especially, for example, when the mother has incurred expense hiring a lawyer and here's the judge speaking kindly to her ex who's clearly a nutbar. She looks and feels resentful. Worse, when he doesn't know the rules or statutes, the judge will tell him! She thinks, 'I have to pay for that and here he is getting it from the judge for free.' Her resentment is apparent from the bench.

To be fair is not an aspirational quality for a judge. It is called for every single day. From the well-dressed and well-behaved to the snivelling, carping, rude individuals who grace the court, all deserve the best the judge has to offer, even the vexatious litigants.

Though for him, I am sometimes tempted to buy a gift —
like an alarm clock that swears instead of ringing. That way
he'll be in for a rude awakening.

24 Community involvement

THROUGHOUT MY TIME on the bench, I have spoken to various community groups about law and the role of a judge.

Often people have come up to me afterwards, somewhat amazed to find I am human. If you don't have much to do with the courts, you can easily conclude that judges are formidable and male. It is always good to crack that particular stereotype.

Often, I have spoken to the over-sixties groups, as they are the most likely to be free to attend daytime meetings. I have found them to be curious about a judge's work, and so I would develop something of a game.

I would outline a scenario.

Say a young woman has been texting while driving. As a result, she crashes into cyclists, killing two and injuring others.

Without any other information, I ask those who think she should go to prison to raise their hands.

Quite a few determined hands go up. Then I add more information, like the victims' family have been part of a restorative justice conference and none of them want her to go to prison.

A couple more hands go down. I speak of her unblemished record.

One more hand disappears. Then I outline the probation report, her employer's glowing comments, her offer of significant reparation.

No hands are left.

To me, it's interesting because without all the facts, we are likely to make flawed decisions. It is easy to judge when you know half the story.

And if I'd, say, brought that young woman to the meeting and they'd had the chance to hear from her directly, I've no doubt that compassion would be foremost. It's easier to damn people in their absence than to be confronted with them face to face and maintain that vengeance is best.

I also liked to play the sentencing game. What do you think is the maximum sentence that a judge can impose for, say, careless driving causing death?

They always start high, some at 10 years.

No one has ever guessed correctly that the maximum is only three months in prison, and/or a fine up to $4500 coupled with mandatory disqualification of licence for six months.

There's a lot of tut-tutting at that. That is when we talk about the court's role to apply the legislation that Parliament has enacted. If you want to play the blame game, turn it on the politicians, not the judges.

These groups are remarkably forgiving people. Maybe it's something about having lived for 60 to 80 years and acquired some wisdom. I don't know. They never strike me as a segment of society baying for blood. If any are, they keep it to themselves.

Often people will come to talk afterwards about their careers as teachers, probation workers, lawyers and so on.

I remember one lady who'd worked in a town teaching all her life. She reckoned you could always tell at kindergarten level if a child was going to turn out to be a bad egg.

One of my colleagues was attending a community work initiative one afternoon when he spied a young person for whom he'd issued an arrest warrant for failing to turn up to court. The judge asked why he hadn't come to court and got the old 'I forgot'. Knowing an arrest on Friday would likely mean he'd spend the weekend in the cells, my sympathetic friend offered him the option of going to court that afternoon. He explained he had no way of getting there.

The judge told him he had two feet and if they were applied in a running-type motion, he could cover the five kilometres in no time. He saw the sense in the judge's suggestion and off he went.

The judge later passed him, wound down his window and helpfully suggested he needed to up his pace. The lad obviously appreciated that, as he waved (or the judge thought it was a wave) and applied the pedal to the metal, arriving at court with a decent bead of sweat and slightly out of breath. The warrant was revoked.

I've also spoken to groups of social workers, teachers and nurses. The one common denominator is their compassion for people, and perhaps that's not surprising given their career choices. They're all looking for the best in people.

Their questions and their stories reflect not a cynicism with humanity but a desire to make things better, to help people heal.

I admire that enormously.

They are the ones at the coalface, the ones more likely to suffer burnout because of the relentless demands of their jobs. For them, I always save my favourite joke, which goes like this.

A social worker was making a mini mental state evaluation of three elderly men in a nursing home. The social worker asked the men, 'How much is three times three?'

The first man responded, 'Fifty-eight!'

The second man answered, 'Tuesday.'

The third man said, 'Nine.'

Surprised, the social worker exclaimed to the third man, 'That's right! How did you come up with that answer?'

The man replied, 'It was easy. I just subtracted 58 from Tuesday.'

Then there are the groups comprising professional people. They want a snappy talk that will inform and amuse. They are invariably tougher on crime. They don't want any namby-pamby waffle about the poor. Give me three takeaway points and a joke I can tell my colleagues later. Time is money, so let's make this count.

Speaking to bankers, I dispense first with the bad joke. 'I hope your careers have more longevity than the first-day bank employee who got fired. A woman asked him to check her balance, so he pushed her over.'

Now we can get down to business.

I give them some Family Court fact scenarios and ask how they would resolve it. Many of them have families. Put them in the hot seat and they think of solutions that would work for them. It's always nice (read gratifying) to stretch their thinking. After all, these people are used to solving problems, albeit financial ones.

Then I talk about my job and the days, especially in the criminal court, when sentences are imposed quickly, in a busy court, one after another.

We talk about the comparisons in our jobs and what makes them different.

I'm tempted to ask them if they remember when nurses, carers, teachers and students crashed the stock market, wiped out banks, took billions in bonuses and paid no tax. No, me neither. But I don't.

With all these groups, it's an enormously rewarding exercise. We don't all think alike. Sometimes there are surprising similarities, but I think the over-sixties could teach the accountants a thing or two and the bankers could learn from the nurses. And we could all learn from each other.

25 Stress

MY DOCTOR TOLD me to start killing people. Well, not in those exact words. She said I had to reduce the stress in my life.

Stress. It seems to be the natural accompaniment to life these days. I stress therefore I am.

There are books and seminars and videos on stress: how to avoid it, overcome it, make friends with it. But the concept of stress hasn't been with us throughout human history. In fact, it was only popularised in the twentieth century, after being coined by Canadian endocrinologist Dr Hans Selye in 1936, to describe a non-specific response of the body to any demand for change.

It was American physiologist Walter Cannon, however, who, in 1915, came up with the term 'fight or flight' to describe an animal's response to threats. He asserted that it was not only physical emergencies but also psychological ones that caused the release of adrenaline into the bloodstream.

More recently, the definition of stress has widened to include our response to any experience or event over which we have little control.

The weekly routine of school pick-ups, soccer practice, dance classes, cooking, cleaning and maintaining healthy relationships can all produce stress. So too can the demands of work, the helplessness of caring for a family member with Alzheimer's, being unemployed. The list is endless.

In court, we may not know the origin of a person's stress, but we see the effects of it in anger, irritability and, sometimes, exacerbated mental health issues. Chronic stress can leave a person unable to see their way out of the fog.

What might have started as workplace redundancy can lead to the body being unable to cope with the constant side-effects of stress, resulting in serious health problems such as heart disease, cancer and depression. And the more we worry, the worse it gets.

For many of those in the court system, stress is a natural companion. I'm not just talking about those facing charges. Court staff, lawyers, judges and those sitting in the public gallery can all have a mental tape running while doing whatever they came to court for.

How do I cope with this? Why is my heart racing? Why do I feel like I'm drowning?

Stress is the trash of modern life, as one American put it. We all generate it, but if we don't dispose of it properly, it will pile up and overtake our lives.

Some 80 to 90 per cent of diseases are believed to be stress related.

There are some jobs in which stress is inevitably part of the job. Take social workers, for instance. They might effect some change, but there's a lot of things they can't overcome, like poverty, intergenerational violence and social inequality.

Palliative nurses are also at high risk of burnout. They can't prevent their patients from dying. At times they are even unable to relieve a patient's physical symptoms.

We all have our burdens. Stress can lead us to make poor decisions, large and small, even when we don't ascribe that to stress. I've seen the stressed witness, nervous of the court process in the first place, who reaches the point where they get completely muddled.

Like the woman who called the airline customer service desk to ask if she could take her dog on board. 'Sure,' was the reply, 'as long as you provide your own kennel.'

He further explained, 'The kennel needs to be large enough for the dog to stand up, sit down, turn around and roll over.'

The woman was completely flummoxed. 'I'll never be able to teach him all that by tomorrow.'

We all must deal with stress. What matters is how we carry it and how we dispose of it. And, first, whether we recognise it.

In 2015, I was carted off to hospital with heart palpitations. I had taken a short adjournment from court, worried I might pass out. That would not have been a good look: lawyers thinking their submissions had finally sent me over the edge or the parties who had waited a year to get into court groaning inwardly at another bloody delay.

After a battery of tests determined that my heart was thumping away just as it should, I was asked about my job. Was it stressful? Just a bit. Did I work more than 40 hours a week? Hell, yes. Did I exercise? Well, I walked from my chambers to court a few times a day.

It was stress pure and simple.

I learned that I could ignore the warning signs at my peril. I started meditation, more walking and getting regular massages. For me, reading poetry has always been a great soother. Mary Oliver, Alice Walker, May Sarton and our own Brian Turner, Hone Tuwhare and James K. Baxter provided the *sangfroid* I was after that helped restore some balance.

When I felt less stressed, my sense of humour returned. I believe a sense of humour is essential for a judge. We can take ourselves too seriously. The job might require tact and objectivity, but humour helps keep your feet on the ground.

Like the seriously frazzled one who said, 'I've been feeling really stressed lately, so my doctor advised me that before going to bed, I should drink two glasses of red wine, after a

hot bath, but to be honest, it's not really helping at all . . .
I can't even finish drinking the hot bath water.'

Humour also keeps you going through the tough dry
patches, remembering who you are and honouring that.

As Camus said, in the midst of winter, I discovered
that there was in me an invincible summer. I needed to
rediscover that too.

I believe, without any objective evidence to support it,
that women are more prone to doubt and falling prey to that
old fraud complex mentality than men. Women judges are in
a decided minority. No matter how convinced we are of our
invincible summer, there is also lurking in the background
the fear that one day someone will discover we are no good.

I've talked to men about this. Sure, they have doubts, but
usually not the deep-down imposter fraud syndrome that
besets women. It is something to do with the painful and
often slow road to success.

It's also about believing those voices in our heads that
constantly belittle us with the nasty put-downs. It was
Eckhart Tolle who helped me with that one when he wrote:
what a liberation to realise that the 'voice in my head' is not
who I am. Who am I then? The one who sees that.

I once attended a week-long litigation skills programme
when I was a lawyer. These programmes are run by the
New Zealand Law Society and are excellent for upskilling.
Cross-examination is recorded and played back to analyse
every empty hand gesture, stammer and facial tic. Lawyers
take part in a trial with real judges. Volunteers play the role
of jurors.

It can be challenging.

One thing stood out from all the memories of those
programmes I attended, as a lawyer and later as a judge. I
was paired up with a young woman lawyer. We got to know
each other as the week progressed.

One day we were talking about our fears.

Hers was a precise description of the fraud complex. This

from a woman who had been dux of her school, won the award for best student at law school, was readily accepted into one of the top Auckland law firms, and had just returned from the UK where she had completed a post graduate degree at Oxford.

Deep down she believed that one day *they* would find out that she wasn't really that capable. Sounds crazy, right? If someone with that level of ability can be beset by the fraud complex, what hope is there for the rest of us?

By the time you arrive on the bench, or at that vaunted position you have always wanted, you wonder if you deserve it.

That can lead to working harder to prove your worth. And the working harder leads to stress. And stress can lead to fatal heart attacks or strokes.

You do not want to be the person for whom your sole purpose in life is to simply serve as a warning to others.

The answer? As writer Anne Lamott put it, almost everything will work again if you unplug it for a few minutes — including you.

26 Racism

IF POVERTY AND unemployment are endemic in New Zealand, racism is right up there too.

From casually racist comments to outright prejudice, discrimination can start small. The taunts at school, the assumptions in the workplace, the casual bias in literature and history provide a lens through which we view life, and that is often coloured by fear. Fear that 'they' are different from us and therefore inherently dangerous.

Some commentators display breathtakingly racist views which spit out from talkback radio, Facebook and newspaper columns. Michael Laws is one such example with his observation on the Treaty of Waitangi, which he described as 'a rat-nibbled, irrelevant straightjacket'.[54] Yet this document is enshrined in most New Zealand legislation, passed by politicians of all political colours, as fundamental to our heritage. In this way, the Treaty has transcended the original document to serve contemporary New Zealand society. To attempt to relegate it as irrelevant does little for our race relations.

It is hard to believe that the proud city of Dunedin might have been so afraid of Chinese immigrants that, in 1888, they passed a unanimous resolution which effectively made it more difficult for Chinese newcomers to live there. A poll tax was imposed on them, which was not repealed until 1944.

We are coming to terms, albeit slowly, with the institutional racism that beset Māori from the time European settlers established their communities here. While Māori had political standing in Parliament from 1867 with four seats, and inter-race marriage was generally accepted, it was land that proved to be the catalyst for a deep and abiding racism. The New Zealand Wars of 1845 to 1872, themselves triggered mostly by disputed land sales, were followed by large-scale land confiscations as a convenient punishment imposed by the victors. This, combined with the many other means of alienation, meant the land was lost to Māori, along with their right of access to harvest food as before.

If that was bad, the push for Māori to assimilate meant compulsory English only in classrooms, depriving many not only of their language but of their culture, often perceived as backwards. To be forward thinking meant realising that the Pākehā was culturally superior.

Fast-forward to after the Second World War and discrimination took many forms. Māori were at times refused rental accommodation and could be segregated in cinemas. Their drift to the cities saw them out of touch with their local marae and family support, losing not only cultural identity but pride in the process.

The young Māori man who has no idea of his whakapapa and no whānau to stand with him is lost indeed. So too is the Māori wahine who seeks love and security in all the wrong places that produce not a healthy relationship but the scars of domestic violence and six children to go with it.

To grow up with dreams and aspirations, we need to be fed the notion that all things are possible. In our family, my Scots parents would say, 'Ye canna say canna.' You *can* do this.

If all you have known is poverty and indirect or direct racism, it's hard to push through those barriers.

A prominent Hamiltonian told me of the challenges

his son faced. They were a Māori–Pākehā couple whose son was a medical student. Countless times he would be stopped by police, and often it appeared to him it was for no other reason than he was brown and therefore, by definition, a potential troublemaker. If white lads were stopped as regularly, there would be trouble.

Or take the recent example of a black barrister in England on a normal working day. Three times she was mistaken for a defendant, the assumption being she was black and therefore couldn't possibly be a professional.[55]

On a fairly frequent basis, we judges would attend seminars, designed specifically to challenge us about racism. We'd hear stories from those whose lives had been blighted by it. We would visit maraes and be coached in Te Reo. We learned the statistics and facts on racism in New Zealand. Yes, some of that is armchair learning and yes you could say we returned to our comfortable lives. Whether we were touched by what we learned is always for the individual judge to determine.

For me it was pivotal. I'd look at a Māori defendant about to be sentenced and ask myself: would I treat him the same as the last person in the dock who was white and supported by a middle-class-looking family?

There is an inherent racism deep within us that casually writes people off.

Asian drivers.

On-the-dole Māori.

Immigrants on benefits.

Indian curry munchers.

The list goes on.

Attitudes, however, can be challenged by law change.

The Waitangi Tribunal was established in 1975 to make recommendations on claims brought by Māori relating to Crown actions which breach promises made in the Treaty of Waitangi; most often claims relate to land grievances.

Three years before that, in 1972 New Zealand ratified the

International Convention on the Elimination of all Forms of Racial Discrimination intended to outlaw hate speech and to promote and protect human rights.

Since then, the Human Rights Act was passed in 1993, to prevent unfair treatment or discrimination on the grounds of race, creed, gender, and so on.

Until then, a landlord could turn away a prospective Māori tenant, anyone could be denied access to a public place and a woman could see her job disappear once she fell pregnant.

More recently, section 27 of the Sentencing Act 2002 has come into focus. That section allows an offender to ask the court for a report, whether written or oral, on a person's cultural background.

Such reports have rarely been used, despite the 18 years since the act was passed. But if they were called for more often, it may provide the judge with an understanding of an offender's links, or lack of them, to their cultural background, and that can be useful in the rehabilitative aspect of sentencing. For example, as part of a supervision sentence, an offender can be directed to attend and complete a Tikanga Māori programme, to learn more about their iwi and hapū, and about their culture and history.

Some would argue that Māori cannot get a fair trial in New Zealand, because institutional racism is so imbedded in our culture that a jury are more likely to convict a Māori than, say, a Pākehā.

That argument was one of the planks advanced in a 2020 appeal against conviction for murder. The 22-year-old Māori woman had no previous convictions and was found guilty of killing her partner.

In the Court of Appeal,[56] her lawyer said his client was Māori by descent and appearance. No safeguard was put in place to lessen the racial prejudice that jurors may have had against her, simply because she was Māori. The New Zealand Bill of Rights Act gives everyone charged with an offence 'the right to a fair and public hearing' and, under section 19, the right of freedom from discrimination.

Her lawyer asserted that failure to guard against the illegitimate effects of jury prejudice had given rise to a miscarriage of justice.

The Court of Appeal rejected that argument but did repeat the observations made in another case three years earlier, also in the Court of Appeal. There, the judge said:

'There is ample research which shows that unconscious bias exists, though (for those not negatively affected) it is rarely obvious and often overlooked. Few who discriminate on the basis of race will admit it. Some will prefer to hide it. Most will be unaware of it and so will find the suggestion they do so insulting.

'Racial bias finds expression in policing as it does in other parts of the community. An internal survey of frontline police officers (independently conducted for the New Zealand police and Te Puni Kōkiri) concluded that, while cultural awareness within police was improving, racially biased attitudes persisted in a minority of officers. While this study is more than 15 years old, the disparity in "criminal justice outcomes" that triggered concerns explored in it and other studies remains unchanged, and in some respects has become worse.'[57]

Many are critical of the present justice system for all kinds of reasons. There are those who complain of sentences being too light or for a failure to adequately treat those who have addiction issues. But there are increasingly louder voices who hold that the system is racist and bewildering for those trying to navigate its corridors.

In 2020, the Safe and Effective Justice Advisory Group[58] produced a report calling for transformative change to the justice system.

The report writers interviewed many people. Those who are harmed by and cause violence, along with community groups, police and those who work in the courts, spoke of how the justice system is failing victims and perpetrators.

Sixty-three per cent of respondents in a 2018 victim survey said their experience of the criminal justice system was poor or very poor.

The Advisory Group's report also makes intelligent proposals for change, and it notes that to achieve that change will require the involvement of all of us. Specifically, it calls for courage, clarity of purpose, investment in communities and people, and a willingness to share power.

It's not accidental that the title of the report, *Turuki! Turuki!*, is a rallying cry to the crew of a waka, or to anyone trying to move a large inert object. It is a call for collective action.

One of the lesser-known initiatives involves the 15 Rangatahi Courts, Ngā Kōti Rangatahi, for youth offenders. They are dotted around New Zealand and were first trialled by Judge Heemi Taumaunu in 2008.

The court meets on a marae and always follows a conventional Youth Court appearance by the young offender. While they are intended to deal primarily with Māori youth, they are open to all ethnicities.

Rangatahi Courts have an emphasis on holding a young person accountable for their offending. At the same time, they introduce the young person to Māori protocol and customs. Each offender must prepare a pepeha, or self-introduction, in Māori and are appointed a lay advocate to help them research their family background.

It is well known that young Māori who are disconnected from their heritage are disproportionately represented in the Youth Court and later in prison. Addressing that and holding them accountable are the keys to change. But they are not the whole answer.

The responsibility for change rests with us all. At a grass-roots level, the racist joke, the attitude that writes them all off as lazy or violent, do nothing to inhibit the spread of a way of thinking that creates an 'us' and 'them' divide.

It's those microaggressions that are habit forming, the everyday acts of intolerance and discriminatory treatment.

They may seem small or insignificant, but to those on the receiving end, they can cause a build-up of despair and victimisation.

Take, for example, young Mohammed at school. He looks different, is still struggling with English and the cultural norms he is growing up with are very different from Kiwi ones. The schoolground taunts, the rude comments he hears walking with his mother to school, become ingrained.

The same with Hemi who, all through his schooling, has never been encouraged to be a doctor or writer. Neither his family nor neighbours see him as a star in the making. On the contrary, it's said he's 'that Māori boy', 'the loser', 'he'll never amount to much'.

He will come to believe it, and our society will be the poorer for it because we'll never know the heights he could have reached if he'd received the message over and over again that he is somebody, not nobody.

Nelson Mandela said it well. No one is born hating another person because of the colour of his skin, or his background, or his religion. People must learn to hate and if they can learn to hate, they can be taught to love, for love comes more naturally to the human heart than its opposite.

27 Witness reliability

WHEN I WAS A NEW JUDGE, along with other newbies I attended a seminar on judicial security. Our partners were also invited, since our protection was a matter of equal interest to them. We were all sitting around a large table, when suddenly two masked men burst in, told us not to look at them, shouted orders, swore and left. After we'd all recovered our equilibrium, which took a while, we were asked to record some information, such as what colour hats they wore, what they said, whether either had any distinguishing marks, and so on.

We were terrible! Hats were a range of colours, while one judge was certain neither wore hats. On the subject of what was said, one could only remember a torrent of 'fuck youse'.

In retrospect, though not at the time, I found that exercise interesting. How revealing that we, trained as lawyers to be careful and objective, were all at sea when it came to a united voice as witnesses. Yes, it came out of the blue, but so does a bank robbery or car crash.

Put us on the spot, and what we're so sure about in our recall can become murky with the shock of it, or the passage of time, or comparing stories with others.

Witness reliability. In fact, we are notoriously unreliable when it comes to giving evidence about what we saw or heard.

In the United States, the Innocence Project has charted convictions that were subsequently overturned by DNA evidence. Of 21 overturned in 2011, 19 were based on eyewitness testimony.

Some states do not allow DNA testing to be carried out after a conviction to test the veracity of that conviction, but where that has occurred, the Project's statistics on the number exonerated by DNA since 1989 are significant. There have been 367, and of those 69 per cent involved eyewitness misidentification.

In the UK, it's estimated that up to 100 people are wrongly convicted each year because of false eyewitness testimony.

Experiments were conducted at the University of Huddersfield on volunteers who watched footage of a bar fight. Actors were planted as dummy eyewitnesses suggesting the wrong man started the fight. Where the actors were present, the mistake rate went as high as 95 per cent. Leave out the actors and that reduced to 32 per cent. So what people thought they saw was easily influenced and distorted by comments from others.

In 1999, the New Zealand Law Commission produced a paper on the reliability of witness testimony. In it, they noted that human memory is fragile and subject to change.

They described how eyewitness recall can be flawed because of either inherent human cognitive limitations or the ways in which information is drawn from eyewitnesses.

I have sat on cases in both the Family Court and criminal jurisdiction when it was difficult to determine if a witness was telling the truth. Sometimes it is obvious. But where a witness is cohesive and calm in their retelling, who's to say they're not an outright liar or a very honest individual?

Cultural practices can play a part. Pacific Islanders

are generally quietly spoken with head down in court. It is often a mark of respect but can be misinterpreted as evasive behaviour.

Then there are those who give it all away before they even get to court. Like the wanna-be bank robber who burst into a bank and yelled, 'This is a hold-up! Everyone on the ground.'

He looked around then said, 'Aw, not you, Aunty.'

That from one of our own Kiwis in a real-life scenario, where identification of the bank robber turned out to be a breeze.

Those who take longer to answer or seem forgetful can be deemed unreliable, when in fact all that's happening is that they are slower to recall what might be completely accurate.

I don't place too much store by the idea that if a witness looks up and to the left, they are telling the truth, to the right they are lying. Nor does body language necessarily indicate a lie. A witness who often scratches their face may just have an itch or a nasty skin condition. Another who constantly looks to the courtroom door may just want out!

We are used to judging people's mannerisms and drawing conclusions. He yawns loudly. He must be bored. She raises her eyebrows. She doesn't believe a word you're saying. Yet the social scientists tell us that in the court setting a certain demeanour is not a good indicator of lying, notwithstanding those TV programmes like *Lie to Me*. They make for good entertainment but not great science.

One commentator has described the Othello error. This occurs when a witness is nervous while being cross-examined. The error is the false interpretation of the stress of it all as insincerity.

On the other side of the coin is the halo effect, where a judge might see a witness in good or bad terms and that impression will colour all other judgment. Once the impression is formed, it attaches to all the evidence of a witness, regardless of their testimony.

Describing these features in an article, retired High Court

Judge Robert Fisher QC concluded: 'The one source that cannot be usefully resorted to is demeanour. Judges and other factfinders should keep this in mind when listening to evidence.'[59]

Of course, there is the witness who gives themselves away. Like the man brought in by the family as a witness on their behalf. He was a self-described healer. He could heal anyone!

Unfortunately, when he finished his evidence, he asked to be lifted out of the witness box as he couldn't manage on his own.

A judge must gather up *all* the evidence. What a witness says and how they say it must be evaluated with the rest of the case.

Turns out the old song about lyin' eyes is as reliable as looking to the left or right.

I remember meeting a child in my chambers. She was present with her lawyer and very vocal about her life, what she liked and disliked about her parents.

I was trying to decide which parent she should live with. She told me who her friends were, what subjects she liked at school, and the pets she had. In particular we discussed her pet turtle Shelley, who could cross the road, slowly, who ate lettuce and liked being taken to school to meet the other children.

Back in court, I recounted to her parents the conversation we'd had. I told them of her fondness for Shelley, and they stared back blankly at me. Turned out there was no turtle! I simply could not tell the difference between the story of her friends at school (true, said her lawyer) and the turtle (totally false). Deluded by a kid.

I recall another story involving a child who was taken by the social worker to the doctor after receiving neck injuries that were deemed non-accidental. The doctor enquired of the child, 'And how did this happen?'.

'I got bitten by a crocodile', the little girl replied.

Witnesses do get flustered in court. They know what they mean to say, but something quite different comes out.

Like the witness who left an altercation at his house, jumped into his car, raced off and was promptly hit by another vehicle. As he put it, 'I went from the fire into the frying pan.'

Or the witness answering the question 'What is your date of birth?'

'July 1st.'

'What year?'

'Every year.'

I have had a witness in court refusing to answer a question, saying, 'I take the Fifth.' I think he had been watching too much American TV.

The witness brought in by the defence to bolster a case can be a total disaster when their recall has done an about-turn.

I had one trial in which the defendant was trying to assert he was nowhere near the late-night tussle which evolved into a pitched battle with two other men. His evidence was that he was miles away. His mate Pete would vouch for that.

But Pete failed to come up to brief as they say. His evidence of the defendant's injuries, coupled with who said what to whom before it all started, effectively put the case to bed. Guilty.

It can be risky for a lawyer to call a witness when you don't know what the witness will say. In fact, it's never advisable. But the lawyer assisting the court is in a tricky position, especially as sometimes occurs in the Family Court. A self-represented woman, described by some as mad as a snake, insisted on her friend being called as a witness.

He duly arrived, wearing Stubbies shorts, and marched to the witness box. When asked, he refused to sit. He was quivering with aggression.

The judge used her best mother voice: 'Would you please state your name?' He looked around the court.

'No, I'm not saying a fucken thing until youse have all

introduced yourselves.' They did, one by one like obedient children, but his evidence only confirmed that he too was as mad as a snake.

I confess to employing that old human instinct, intuition.

First impressions are not necessarily accurate, but over the course of a trial or in the Family Court, reading endless affidavits, and meeting the parties several times, you can develop a sense of where justice lies.

That is not to say there's no need for conscious reasoning, but just saying.

28 Is it hard to decide?

SOMEONE ONCE ASKED ME what it was like making decisions about people's lives. Do you angst over them? Are you awake at 3 a.m. wondering if you got it right?

A decision to remove a child from her mother or send a young man to prison for the first time is undoubtedly huge.

It's not done in a vacuum, though. It is hedged by either a trial or a guilty plea. In the Family Court, the judge hears evidence from parents, interested parties, a psychologist, sometimes a social worker and, of course, a meeting with the child.

In almost all cases, the outcome is clear after weighing up all the evidence. What a judge doesn't have is hindsight or the ability to see the future. No one does. We do the best with the information we have at the time.

Have I ever got it wrong? Yes.

Have I ever regretted a decision? Yes.

Have I ever got it absolutely right? Yes.

You do the best you can. You apply the law scrupulously, consider the evidence carefully. You weigh up one factor against another. You apply your legal training and come to a decision. If you get it wrong, any one of at least three things may happen.

First, your decision is appealed and either overturned or upheld.

Second, the affected parties go away and live with the changes of childcare or the young person sent off to prison, and you never get to know what the outcome of that decision was on all concerned.

Third, you hear later, sometimes anecdotally, that the care arrangements became a disaster, or that the young man really learned Criminal 101 in prison and, on being released, went on to kill someone.

The 1998 movie *Sliding Doors* stays with me as an example of the way a storyline can be played out in two different ways, with moments that can alter the trajectory of your life.

I don't mean to suggest that judging is happenstance — far from it. As I've said, it's a carefully thought-through exercise of applying law to the facts.

Decision making is something we all have to do, and no one gets it bang on all the time. Poet Rudyard Kipling was right when he said, in his poem 'If': 'If you can meet with Triumph and Disaster / And treat those two imposters just the same.' Because what may seem like failure isn't necessarily so. The same goes for success.

I once made a decision in the Family Court concerning a young lad who didn't get on with his dad and didn't want to continue the week-about care arrangement. His parents slugged it out in court. While the matter was finely balanced, I favoured the status quo. I was a little suspicious that Mum was behind the son's dissatisfaction with Dad. I felt, given time, things may come right.

I was wrong.

Not many months after my decision insisting the 11-year-old maintain his time with his dad, the boy voted with his feet. He climbed out the bedroom window, walked a considerable distance to Mum's and thereafter refused to see his father — at all.

How would this have played out if I had acquiesced to the son's wish, even to a limited degree? Success or failure, who knows?

The other factor in all of this is life. I remember a competition in which the first prize went to the person who could, among other words, spell 'Qantas'. A young woman spelled it 'Quantas' and came second. Her prize was a trip in a plane up in the cockpit and she was so captivated by that experience that she went on to train as a Qantas pilot. I don't know what the first-prize winner won or did thereafter, but I have always seen that story as an apt metaphor for life.

We simply do not know what first or second prize will bring us, or even coming last. Life intervenes, takes our successes and our failures and does something inexplicable with them.

While I do not mean to imply that we are helpless creatures of fate, I do believe we must make our decisions as best we can and then leave the outcome for another day.

Yes, I have lain awake at 3 a.m. before and after delivering a decision, turning it over in my mind, looking at it from all angles, agonising about the outcome.

I have also driven home from work, barely able to see the road in front of me for the flood of tears. I have done that on at least three occasions. Once after hearing a victim impact report of horrendous abuse. Once after having to review pornographic images involving children. And once after being obliged to sentence a woman to a lengthy term of imprisonment. She was on her second-strike offence, so the years I imposed were what she would serve, without any time off for good behaviour.

Is it hard to decide? At times immeasurably so. Some could say, well, that's what you are paid to do. Quite right. But the question wasn't posed to me in terms of would you rather not decide, rather, how does it feel when you do — what if it is wrong?

Until I became a judge, I used to think such people were

individuals with super-high IQs, with brains larger than the rest of us and genius to boot. I know, I know.

After I became a judge, I realised they were mere mortals *but* with an ability to think logically and dispassionately. It's not the IQ that makes a good judge, but rather being able to make a decision taking all the facts and law into account.

It takes a certain bravery, in any court, to make a decision that may run against public opinion, whether it be considered too harsh or too light. Bravery too in any decision I suspect. We, all of us, must make decisions that are, at times, unpopular.

The parents of any teenager know that. So too does the employer in times of redundancy, and the children of an elderly parent reluctantly facing rest-home options.

Hard decisions must be made, and they can mount up and overwhelm us. As a judge, I always found it easier when I had one reserved decision to write. I could ruminate about it, toss it around in my mind and reflect on all the competing arguments. But when they piled up, two, three or four, then the pressure was on, and the decision was harder to construct and finish.

A study at Columbia University found that most Americans have, on average, 70 conscious decisions to make in each day.[60] Consequently, the study authors concluded it is easy to suffer from decision fatigue. The Jam Study[61] is a case in point.

In 2000, shoppers at a food market were presented with 24 varieties of gourmet jam. Those who tried the jam received a coupon for $1 off any jam. On another day, shoppers were offered the choice of only six jams. While the large display attracted more interest, when it came time to buy, people were much more likely to purchase from the small display. The message was excessive choice can produce 'choice paralysis'.

I didn't know about the Jam Study at the time, but I knew that when more decisions were piling up, it made the job harder.

Having made the decision, you cannot second-guess it. It is a bit like the old saying, 'You made your bed, you lie in it'. That's usually accompanied by a thin-lipped, I told-you-so kind of censorious disapproval. Or maybe that's just me, when I think of that line.

Anyway, the upshot is decisions are hard in or out of court. I don't mean what will I wear today, or is it going to be sushi or Subway for lunch? Deciding about people's lives is complicated and messy and I think it's good to remember that.

I have always tried to keep at the forefront of my mind the awareness that it is a person's life I am dealing with and the ramifications of my decision spread like ripples in a pool. It affects the spouse, children, the grandparents, friends and neighbours. It plays out over years. It changes people's options and choices. I am under no illusion about that. I have never made a decision lightly.

But once it's done, it's done. In the judicial system, there are very few ways of taking a decision back. If it contains a pertinent error, it can be recalled by consent with all the parties. Clerical errors can be corrected. Beyond that, you live with what you decide.

As Napoleon Bonaparte once opined, nothing is more difficult, and therefore more precious, than to be able to decide.

Besides, if you have never got it wrong, you have never made a decision.

29 Where there's a will

WHEN I WAS A LAWYER, one piece of advice I often handed out was 'get a will'. It's surprising how many people, including lawyers and judges, haven't got around to it, have forgotten or don't realise their will is invalid. Divorce changes your legal status, so for any subsequent nuptials, you need not only a partner but also a new will.

It's not hard. There's plenty of advice online about how to draw up a will, which is basically who you want to leave your stuff to. It must be witnessed and here's a trap for young players, like me starting out as a lawyer.

I was asked to visit a man in hospital after our firm had drawn up his will. He clearly wasn't long for this world but was alert and lucid. I found a cleaner willing to be a witness, got it signed and returned to the office. My supervising partner checked it and gently pointed out I had obtained only one witness signature. Big mistake! I nearly passed out on the spot, worried my man would die before I got back to him. Fortunately, he hung in there and his will was duly signed and witnessed by two people. Neither of them can be someone named in the will, so the witnesses must be independent.

Sometimes people arrange to draw up a living will, dealing with instructions for resuscitation or medical care in the event they become unconscious. That is to be contrasted with an ordinary will, which only takes effect on death.

If you think you don't have much stuff to leave, think again. Grandma's set of silver spoons may not have enormous value on Trade Me, but a couple of cousins may have their eyes on them, creating all sorts of fuss after she has gone.

Then there's the young bloke with only $5 to his name, who wins Lotto and subsequently gets run over by an articulated truck. Or the mother of four estranged children who often goes scavenging in op shops and brings home an old painting one day, depicting an early New Zealand scene. She has never bothered with a will, since she'd have to spell out that she wants to leave her few worldly goods to a cat home. But after her death, an eagle-eyed daughter claims the painting. She's curious about the painter, gets it valued and word gets out it is seriously valuable. The fight's on.

The children end up in court where they traverse the warm and loving relationship they had with their mother, or if that won't wash, then rely on the provisions of the Family Protection Act.

Section 4 of the act is key. That says, in part, that if the deceased has not made adequate provision for a claimant's proper maintenance and support, the court may, at its discretion, correct that.

Over the years, there have been many court cases where the court has had to decide what 'adequate' and 'proper' mean and how far the discretion can be exercised.

It's a sad but legally interesting area of the law, and I've made many decisions in situations like daughters not provided for when the family farm passed to the son, or unreasonable restrictions on provisions, family members left out in favour of a close neighbour, children from the first marriage losing to the second wife, and so on.

In one interesting case, a claimant, unknown to the family, popped up after the bachelor uncle's death. It turned out the deceased had fathered a child and, back in 1970, signed a child maintenance agreement which had been lodged with a lawyer and provided the necessary evidence of the son's existence after the uncle's unexpected death.

That kind of discovery can provide surprise too at the earlier stage when the will is read. I like the cartoon where the lawyer is dutifully reading as the family gather anxiously in front of the desk:

'To my idle children, I leave the pleasure of having to earn a living.

'To my wife's mistress, I leave my boyfriend, Geoff.

'And to my loyal solicitor, I leave a vast and complex trust guaranteed to be eaten up with legal fees.'

In life, we are generally kind to our relatives. We wouldn't think of asking them for sums of money or their valuable business shares, and if we don't get on with Auntie Maisie, well, we simply ignore her.

After death, it's a different story. Chattels are stripped from the house, while she's still warm, a real estate agent is brought in to work out what a share might be worth. There's a scramble to tot up her total estate and fight over the provisions of her will.

Auntie Maisie was no fool. She'd anticipated a fracas and not only did she leave a will but also a handwritten document spelling out precisely why young Bobbie won't get a bit and Sharon only a little. That can be hard for the lawyer informing the family. It's even harder in court, where everyone expects to have their challenge heard but haven't given a lot of thought to the ultimate legal bill. It's not sufficient to claim Auntie Maisie wasn't fair. A self-represented party won't know about all those court cases that have gone before and why the trifecta of cases[62] in this area of the law are so crucial to a claim.

There has been a great deal of debate at academic, Law

Commission and judicial levels about whether a person making a will should be free to dispose of their property, however unfair or bizarre.

On the one hand, you might say Auntie Maisie raised her children well. She worked hard during her lifetime and her adult children should fend for themselves, and if one is a millionaire and another a pauper, well, that's life.

Others would say, as the law does in broad terms, that a parent has an obligation to provide, although the extent of that obligation is determined by several factors. Was the deceased abusive in their lifetime? Did the claimant try to be a loving child into adulthood? What are the financial circumstances of the claimant?

One thing is certain. You can't ignore the family — and leave it all to that nice young man who has been mowing the lawns for the past few months — without inviting a claim.

If you have no children or relatives, however, you might want to follow Luis Carlos de Noronha Cabral de Camara's example. He was a Portuguese aristocrat, hence the many names. He had no dependants and so his novel approach was to choose beneficiaries from the Lisbon phone book, by random selection. After he died some 13 years later, the beneficiaries were located and told of their windfall. Some thought it a hoax. Well, you would, wouldn't you? But no, the bequests were honoured.

Now there's no malice in a will like that, but as much as I admire William Shakespeare, I do not think the bard did the right thing by his wife. To his daughter went most of his estate while his wife Anne Hathaway only got his 'second best bed'. That, in my view, was shabby.

Not much better was the German poet Heinrich Heine, who was a fan of Shakespeare and named two of his poems after Bill: 'A Midsummer Night's Dream' and 'A Winter's Tale'. He had married a 19-year-old shop assistant and although they remained together until his death 15 years later, his will grudgingly left all to her on the one condition she remarry so 'there will be at least one man to regret my death'. But if you think that's harsh, what follows on a will being challenged is often worse.

I remember one case involving the second wife and the adult children of the first marriage. Of course, the second wife was seen as the proverbial wicked stepmother and the adult children were no doubt delighted when the second marriage hit the rocks. At that point, the husband changed his will, leaving out his wife. He developed cancer just weeks later. While in hospital, a reconciliation took place. Then he died, presumably not knowing what a mess he'd left to sort out.

Tensions were high. Guns would have been drawn at dawn in a different era.

The deceased's ashes were divided, a portion to each party. The wife was so angry about it all, she threatened to flush her share down the toilet.

The mediated settlement was a lose–lose all round and not my finest hour as an arbitrator of the dispute.

I used to think that custody battles brought out the worst in people, until I presided over a few will disputes. One of the reasons that wills are contested is because house prices have risen astronomically. That old tumbling-down family home just might fetch a million or two.

Take the scenario where after Mum dies, Dad stays on in the house for another 30 years. His cooking skills aren't great and his house-cleaning efforts are non-existent. He's grumpy and isolates himself. He doesn't take too kindly to advice and it has been a year or more since he changed the sheets. Even worse, he's a hoarder and the newspapers pile up everywhere along with receipts and rat droppings and half-eaten food.

You get the picture.

But this is a house in Ponsonby, Auckland and suddenly the picture changes. It's worth fighting over.

In the United Kingdom in 2019, there were 188 cases

involving contested wills.[63] That was up 47 per cent on the year before. When you realise many disputes never even get to a hearing, the number of those challenging a will is escalating.

So, what's the answer? Spend it all before you die — or spell out your reasoning so clearly that any challenge will shrivel up and die. Like the lawyer reading the will to the many relatives gathered:

'To my son Jim, I leave my house and chattels.

'To my daughter Dot, all my shares.

'To my friend Harry, my ride-on mower.

'And to my cousin Clyde, who always sat around and never did anything, but wanted to be remembered in my will, I say, "Hi, Clyde".'

30 Judicial independence

JUDGES ARE INDEPENDENT. That means they must make their decisions free of influence. There's no good turning up to court waving a wad of money, hoping to be dealt with more leniently. That just won't wash.

Why is it so important? Because people who go to court must do so in the knowledge that the judge hasn't been swayed by the latest newspaper headlines or influenced by some Facebook post.

To be independent, free from bribery or the taint of prejudice is vital. 'I may not like your politics or your personal views, but you'll get a fair treatment in my court' must be the catchcry of every judge.

I venture to suggest that an independent judiciary is the hallmark of justice wherever you are in the world, except maybe for places like China, where in 2017 the Supreme Court President denounced the idea of judicial independence, reminding people that the court is not independent of the Communist Party, which always has the final say.[64] Exceptions aside, is judicial independence really a reality in countries that claim to operate under that principle?

Let's look at whether a court may bring a criminal case

against a person and then sit as judge and jury on that person and would that constitute judicial independence. In New Zealand it is the police or the Crown who lay the charge and then always a judge, independent of them all, who hears the matter.

In India, by contrast, the Supreme Court in one instance laid the charge, heard the matter and convicted the defendant, all, it should be said, after the local police had declined to take any action.[65] It is difficult to see this as an example of judicial independence at work. The facts are these.

Arundhati Roy is an Indian author who won the Man Booker Prize in 1997 with her novel *The God of Small Things*. She is also an activist and environmentalist who fell foul of the Indian court when she criticised a court decision approving the building of a dam in Gujarat. Not just any dam but one that would displace hundreds of thousands of people from their ancient homeland.

Initially, the court decided that, while her words were actionable, they would take it no further. She then took part in a protest outside the court against increasing the height of the dam, whereupon the Supreme Court initiated contempt proceedings against her and three others. In her affidavit, she reiterated what she had said earlier, namely that 'As a free citizen of India I have the right to be part of any peaceful dharna, demonstration or protest march. I have the right to criticise any judgment of the court that I believe to be unjust.'[66]

The court disagreed and sentenced her to one day in prison and a fine.

I suspect the judges took umbrage at being criticised.

Here in New Zealand, it's not a good look to rubbish a judge. In Australia, you're likely to be prosecuted. That said, Australian judges have been variously described as 'feral', 'pathetic', 'a crowd of basket weavers', 'needing a good-behaviour bond' and 'self-appointed Kings and Queens'.[67] Criticism of judges has been fierce and although the law remains in place about scandalising the judiciary being an offence, such comments rarely lead to charges being laid.

In the United Kingdom, since 2013 the door has been opened to criticism of judges by repealing the offence of 'scandalising the judiciary'. So the MP who described a High Court judge as being, among other things, 'off his rocker' was admonished by the Chief Justice who said it was 'highly regrettable', but no charges followed.[68]

Nor did another UK judge take action when a defendant blurted out during a hearing, 'You're a humourless automaton. Why don't you self-destruct?' His Honour merely smiled.[69]

The media in the UK have become increasingly rabid in their denunciation of judges' decisions. As one judge put it, 'In the UK, senior judges are labelled "Enemies of the People" in the mainstream media, and the government does nothing to defend the judiciary.'

What about criticism of our judges? Does it impact on judicial independence if, for example, there is a call to have a judge removed? That was the substance of a critique in 2017.

The judge had discharged a man without conviction after he assaulted his wife, children and the wife's friend. The wife and her friend had exchanged a text about their love for each other. The judge said it was a 'nasty assault', but it had to be seen in context, adding, 'Really this is a situation that does your wife no credit and it does [her friend] no credit. There would be many people who would have done exactly what you did, even though it may be against the law to do so.'

Auckland barrister and journalist Catriona MacLennan commented in the *New Zealand Herald* about the judge's observations, saying he should not be sitting on the bench and by his words had effectively condoned domestic violence. Subsequent to that, the National Standards Committee of the New Zealand Law Society commenced an investigation into whether Ms MacLennan had undermined the dignity of the judiciary and failed to comply with her lawyer's obligation to uphold the rule of law.

Perhaps the committee had had a rush of blood to the head in the first place ... The upshot was Ms MacLennan filed her response and the committee took no further action, saying they believed she had shown an 'objective foundation' for the statements she made. Moreover, police appealed the decision and the High Court on granting the appeal also observed that the judge's comments were inappropriate.[70]

What are the take-home points from all this?

First, we must remember that judges are not democratically accountable to Parliament or to the public. They must stand independent and insulated against any undue influence, without fear or favour. Were it otherwise, judges could be bought off by politicians or influenced by the tide of public opinion.

A good example of this occurred in Australia in 1951 at a time when anti-communist sentiments were at an all-time high. The court struck down as unconstitutional the Communist Party Dissolution Act which had been passed by Parliament and endorsed by the electorate. The court was the subject of criticism at the time, but viewed through the lens of time, the legislation was definitely untenable.

Second, we must take care that criticism of judges is not allowed to proceed unchecked. Informed and insightful censure of a judge is one thing. Throwing nasty epithets around and making personal attacks on judges do little to reinforce what is central to our judicial system, namely that we have a rule of law whereby politicians make the law and judges enforce it. If there is unbridled criticism of judges, whether it be by sound bites, Facebook or in the gutter press, the judges' job is made more difficult.

Most judges see more of the underbelly of life than the average person. They are exposed to the saddest of situations. That is their daily diet. Add name calling, personal threats and uninformed criticism and the job is made immeasurably tougher. If being kind is a mantra endorsed by our prime minister, it should extend to us all.

Third, should politicians be able to slag off a judge's decision? Is it wrong for politicians to hide behind parliamentary privilege and say whatever they like?

Politicians, like any member of the public, may disagree with any decision by a judge. But they should exercise a fair degree of caution. In one case, some years after the judge's name suppression decision, subsequent events led two politicians, one the Leader of the Opposition, to say the original decision had clearly been wrong. That galvanised the New Zealand Bar Association, the body representing barristers, into print. Their spokesperson Jonathan Eaton QC said:

'Politicians wading in with bald and hindsight assessments that a judge's decision was wrong is not only unhelpful, it is quite unfair to the judge . . . That years later, facts have changed, leading to a reconsideration of the earlier decision, does not in any sense mean the original decision was wrong.'[71]

Parliamentarians are bound by their code of conduct. To go against that and speak out unwisely drives another nail in the coffin of judicial independence.

Fourth, we must remember that judges cannot respond to outright criticism, no matter how extreme. There is a risk that the public may infer from judges' silence the implication that the criticism was maybe justified, that having got away with it, the public may let rip whenever they choose on some other hapless judge. Almost gone are the days when yesterday's news is today's fish and chip paper. Nasty comments live on through social media and are repeated *ad nauseam*.

A UK judge was once asked informally what he thought of the banner headlines calling the judges who decided the 1987 Spycatcher case 'YOU OLD FOOLS'.[72] I've always thought that writing in capitals was like shouting at someone. Anyway, Lord Templeman smiled and said that judges in England took no notice of personal insults. Although he did not regard himself as a fool, others were entitled to their opinion. How gracious is that?

31 A matter of substance

AND THEN ALCOHOL said put that on Facebook, it's hilarious.

But alcohol was wrong.

So very wrong.

What looks clever, witty and wicked on Saturday night looks simply shabby and sad on Monday morning.

Alcohol and drug abuse often play out on social media and so end up in court as evidence of an incompetent parent or disqualified driver.

Four in five adults consumed alcohol regularly in the 2017–18 year.[73]

Men are twice as likely as women to be hazardous drinkers. Alcohol.org.nz provides plenty of statistics about the effect of our drinking and the social cost. I do not need to repeat them here. All around us are examples of the effects of overconsumption of alcohol.

A friend who recently spent overnight in hospital with heart trouble was in a room with three young people, all admitted separately and all there to detox from a night of binge drinking.

There are a lot of young people who start the

weekend with the sole aim of getting trashed, with all its consequences of unwanted babies, sexually transmitted diseases, car crashes and a fundamental loss of self-respect.

Similarly, drug addiction takes its toll with the social cost of intervention which includes treatment and counselling services, hospital admissions, police, customs and other law enforcement agencies, and of course the courts and prisons.

Substances such as methamphetamine and cocaine are not just the drug of choice for the poor or unemployed. It's not unusual these days to see teachers, doctors and accountants in court on possession charges. While they may have access to drug rehabilitation programmes, not everybody does.

Like poverty and racism, it's not their problem but ours.

Drug addicts steal to buy drugs. Alcoholics drive under the influence and cause carnage on our roads. We're all affected by it.

There are two initiatives I want to speak about where change is happening and it's all down to judges, police volunteers and others who care enough about the problem to be part of the solution.

First, the Alcohol and Other Drug Treatment Court, which has two such courts in Auckland. They're not a soft touch and it's up to the judge as to whether a person is allowed to participate. They are not available for those facing serious charges, such as sexual offending.

They began as a pilot in 2012, intended to break the relentless cycle of drug dependency. Their success rate has meant they are now permanent courts, and more are expected to be added around the country.

When an offender first comes before the court, their photo is taken. By the time they have successfully undertaken an intensive programme of drug testing, mentoring and treatment, they can look very different at completion, one or two years later.

Each person works with a team comprising the judge,

police, court professionals and support workers. Those who successfully graduate are expected to be working and able to carry out their sentence (which has been delayed until all requirements are completed), all monitored by the judge on an ongoing basis.

The programme is limited to 50 participants at a time. A number of treatment providers work with the court. They include the Salvation Army, Odyssey House and Higher Ground, who all offer residential care.

The expectations are high; total abstinence from alcohol/drugs and crime-free living is required. Honesty is demanded. So too are the 23 other points in the contract an offender signs. Yet independent assessments suggest this programme is working. The recidivism rate among those who graduate is low.

New Zealand has taken on board what works in other drug courts around the world. We have also adapted those programmes to suit New Zealand — the drug court includes the role of Pou Oranga, held by a person with a lived experience of recovery and treatment and a knowledge of Māori language and culture.

When a person finally graduates, their achievements are clear.[74]

A woman in a cropped black jacket, red lipstick and straight black bob walks to the front. She has applied to graduate from the programme. The police prosecutor talks of her 'stunning transformation'. It is now time for her to be sentenced.

She has admitted three counts of drink driving. Each time she was twice the legal limit. These were her fourth, fifth, and sixth drink-driving offences. She has also admitted a charge of perverting the course of justice for giving a false identity during yet another drink-driving arrest.

The judge notes she once posed a significant risk to the community but is now entitled to credit for the work she has done over the past 18 months.

Specifically, she has completed a 90-day Salvation Army

programme and other programmes such as driver safety. Testing has revealed evidence of 336 days sober — she passed all of her 250 drug tests. She has attended more than 250 recovery meetings and contributed 220.5 hours of community work, is working full-time and is respected as a role model in her whānau.

The judge imposes 12 months' supervision and wipes all her fines, then smiles at her, saying, 'Be the person we know you are capable of being.'

Another programme which has been implemented in Waitākere, Waikato, Southland and Otago on an entirely voluntary basis is The Right Track. It takes young drivers who are repeat offenders and offers them nine sessions held on midweek evenings and all-day Saturday.

The programme was started in 2007 by a former schoolteacher, John Finch. In an article on the New Zealand Law Society website, he speaks of the practical nature of the programme:[75]

'They listen to volunteer firefighters speak about their experience with road accidents. They listen to the mothers of victims. There are sessions on brain injuries, they hear from the police's serious crash unit, they visit spinal wards and meet people who are paralysed as a result of driving offences and also meet the medical staff who deal with these injured people.'

He says, 'There are also visits to the court, including the cells, viewing a police van, along with observing an actual court sentencing. They participate in a sentencing re-enactment with a real judge, lawyers, court staff and a police prosecutor.'

Attendance at the programme is a once-only opportunity, so if someone reoffends, they cannot be readmitted for another try.

The programme has a 75 to 85 per cent success rate among those who complete it. That extraordinary statistic was confirmed recently by a joint Waikato University/New

Zealand Police/Waikato District Council Evaluation.

It is a testament to all the volunteers involved in the programme that it is such a success story. It is the only independently evaluated driver programme in New Zealand. All results are analysed every two years by police to check reoffending rates.

The programme has gained international recognition for its results in a field where a success rate of 15 to 20 per cent is regarded as successful.

Given the extraordinary outcomes that have been achieved, I do wonder why The Right Track programme has not been picked up by government and rolled out everywhere around the country.

There is plenty of evidence from police, statistics and numerous case studies that this programme is effective in turning bad drivers into safe ones. It targets people who are deemed recidivist offenders on the road.

I have seen those who have completed the programme and come back to court for sentencing, usually facing a mandatory disqualification period as a minimum penalty. Time and again, the police support an application to waive that disqualification because they believe the offender has truly turned around their poor driving practices.

If 75 to 85 per cent of those who complete the programme do not reoffend, here we have a comprehensive answer to those New Zealanders who pose such a risk to the rest of us on our highways.

Safety barriers and advertising campaigns do not even come close in terms of comparative effectiveness. If every person applying for a licence was required to undertake and complete this programme, I've no doubt our appalling road toll would be significantly reduced.

These are but two of the initiatives designed to help and rehabilitate those whose alcohol or drug dependence threatens to derail their lives. If they can be turned around to become productive members of society, surely it is worth the investment.

Both programmes and many others also depend on the work of those who are not paid — indeed I wonder how many New Zealanders are helped by volunteers, that army of helpers who do it for the love of helping, who see their work as addressing *our* problems to be tackled head on.

We can go back over 2300 years to the words of Greek philosopher Aristotle who posed the question: what is the essence of life? His reply: to serve others and to do good. Those who support these programmes are indeed following that mantra.

32 So you want to become a judge?

YOU'VE READ THIS FAR, and you think, yes, that sounds like a job for me. You might be 17 and a bit rudderless at the moment or a lawyer of 50 who feels like she is treading water and needs a new challenge.

If you are starting out in life is it reasonable to write off judging as a possible career? Does your upbringing in South Auckland preclude even dreaming about such a future?

I like the story of the New Zealand Law Society's President, Tiana Epati, who completed her law degree as a young Pasifika student, graduated but couldn't get a job.[76] As she put it, 'I got zero interviews and zero interest.' So, she went waitressing to pay the rent, serving her classmates who were by now lawyers themselves. At this point you may think this is a miserable end to four years of study.

In a lovely example of happenstance, however, she served a group of lawyers one lunchtime and her calm and unruffled manner impressed one Simon Moore. At the time he was a Crown Solicitor. Now he is a High Court judge. He discovered she was looking for a job and gave her his firm's phone number. She rang, applied for the job that was going, but missed out. So, she offered to work there voluntarily for two weeks. After that, they gave her a job.

You may see this story as a depressing example of how hard it is for Māori and Pasifika to make headway in a career such as law, or indeed for a woman. Let's be clear, the statistics do not favour women in the higher echelons of law.

As Winston Churchill said, though, never give up on something that you can't go a day without thinking about.

Let me digress here for a moment. After deciding that working part-time as a judge wasn't really practical and I would have to resign myself to retiring completely, I became quite down. On a scale of 1 to 10, where 10 is exhilaration, I was regularly a 4. Then I read a book called *Big Magic: creative living beyond fear*, by Elizabeth Gilbert.[77]

It was while reading it that I remembered all the family and friends who said I should write about my life on the bench. My reply to each of them was that I wasn't a writer and, besides, we already had one accomplished wordsmith in the family in my husband Mike. Then it became like trying to swat a persistent fly. The idea simply would not leave.

Elizabeth Gilbert tells some lovely stories about ideas she had for writing a book, ideas she couldn't develop at the time and later, when she tried to put them on paper, the genesis of the idea has flown away to someone else. Ideas don't necessarily stick around; they may find inspiration elsewhere if we don't grab them.

We can look back on our lives and see opportunities that have gone begging, or just gone.

Tiana Epati didn't give up and now she is President of the Law Society.

So, what do you need if you want to become a judge? Well, of course, you need a law degree, and you must have been in practice, holding a practising certificate (rather like a warrant of fitness) for at least seven years. It should go without saying that you must know the law and be of good character. Equally, you must have the 'discipline, capacity and insight to act impartially, independently and fairly'. It sounds obvious that, to be a judge, you must be able to be fair, but that is the hallmark of the job. It's no good if you are hyper-critical or intolerant of those who are different.

Assuming you can meet those criteria, here are seven ideas.

The first is get a mentor. We all need encouragement and guidance. Find someone perhaps in your church, a teacher, a trusted friend or a lawyer, who can be a confidant to your dreams and give you emotional support, especially when the going gets tough. They don't have to be familiar with the law, although it helps if they are on the right side of it. Their advice can keep you focused and on track.

They can be cheerleaders from the sideline or, in the case of a professional mentor, help you to avoid the pitfalls in law, steering you to study the right subjects at law school, applying for jobs, changing firms or going out on your own as a barrister. Of course, in time, they can also support your application to be a judge.

Second, join things. As a law student and later a lawyer, it is a good idea to join the Students' Association or District Law Society. That will provide you with contacts and camaraderie. If you are lucky enough to live in Dunedin, you could become part of OWLS, a very wise organisation, otherwise known as Otago Women Lawyers' Society, that is responsible for the annual Ethel Benjamin Address. It began in 1997 and has continued each year with speakers of worldwide renown and a wealth of topics covered at each address. OWLS also offer their members support, friendship and help when it's needed. I speak as a lifelong OWL.

Third, look for opportunities. Maybe you are a lawyer living in a big city. You feel you're not likely to stand out where you are in your quest for elevation to the bench. Perhaps you might move towns or go out on your own as a barrister. If you need to upskill, consider the litigation skills programme I have mentioned elsewhere. Yes, it is a week out of your job, but you will be exposed to tutors, both lawyers and judges, who provide excellent advice on how to improve your courtroom skills.

If you are feeling a bit bold, approach your local judge. Ask what you could do better in court. They will appreciate your willingness to learn and will undoubtedly give you some tips.

Opportunities don't always come wrapped up with a bow. Sometimes we must look for them. As Milton Berle said, if opportunity doesn't knock, build a door. Flippant maybe, but sometimes we must create opportunities, make way for them, give them some house room.

Fourth, work hard. Whatever you do, always give 100 per cent (unless you're giving blood).

Law studies are demanding, as I discovered after getting all As in arts papers and having to settle for Bs in law school. It's not only the reading and retaining information that can be challenging but it's the mindset you have to develop — to think objectively and analytically, to be able to see both sides of an argument. That comes with time and effort.

The writers of all those inspirational self-help books have a constant theme. They emphasise the importance of believing in yourself, because if you do, you are much more likely to be motivated. From that motivation comes the willingness to work hard, harder than you have ever done before.

Stephen R. Covey, the author of *The Seven Habits of Highly Effective People*,[78] said that motivation is a fire from within. If someone else tries to light that fire under you, chances are it will burn very briefly.

The fifth piece of advice is allied to the last. Don't give up. In the words of the Irish proverb, you will never plough a field if you only turn it over in your mind. Do it and keep doing it and don't give up.

When I was at law school, there were times when it seemed too much of a challenge to manage my responsibilities to my three primary school-aged children, my husband, and a law degree. I missed out on doing things with the children because I had to study. But hard as it was,

I knew if I threw it away, I would be forever regretful. Then later, as a lawyer, I found the hours and the effort difficult. Sometimes, I wondered if this was as good as it got. I am eternally grateful that I didn't stop there. Certainly, I could not suspect what was ahead. Being a judge was never part of my five-year plan, primarily because I did not have enough confidence to believe it was possible. Looking back, I can now see a journey that makes much more sense than it did at the time.

It's only if you don't give up and give it time that you can be unstoppable.

Sixth, stop procrastinating. You may have delaying tactics down to a fine art. You tell yourself if good things come to those who wait, isn't procrastination a virtue? You might even be like Douglas Adams who said, 'I love deadlines. I love the whooshing noise they make as they go by'.

But you delude yourself. Putting it off doesn't get it done. And it just builds up and up until it threatens to overwhelm you, or until you do a hurried job to get it done . . . and do it badly.

So, try developing some strategies for tackling those procrastinating tendencies. Start small if you like. But start. It's easy in the field of law to put off writing those submissions or doing that research you don't enjoy. And let's face it, we all put off tasks we don't like. But, ah, the satisfaction in completion.

Recently, I watched the Netflix documentary on the life of Ruth Bader Ginsburg, the former Supreme Court judge in America who was known for her lifelong commitment to the law and her decisions on gender equality and civil rights. I was particularly taken with the way she was willing to burn the midnight oil both in practice and while a judge.

Now to the seventh and last piece of advice for those who would like to become a judge. The process of applying involves an interview, form filling and sending letters of support from friends and colleagues. But here's the thing.

You may not be successful the first time. Don't give up (see above). You should apply more than once.

I have spoken to many judges whose stories of becoming a judge involved a rather convoluted journey. In years gone by, it was more of a phone call from the chief judge asking if you were interested rather than the formal process it has now become. Many are not successful at their first try. Some were interviewed, told yes, then the decision was undone. Others applied and heard nothing. Still others were unsuccessful, put the idea to one side and then received a call sometime later inviting them to consider appointment to a certain town.

Now, the process is intended to be transparent and readily understood. You fill in an application seeking appointment, are interviewed if you are shortlisted and then the successful applicant's name is sent to the Attorney-General for mention at Cabinet and ratification by the Governor-General.

Remember there are several options at the District Court level. You can elect to work in the Youth Court, Family, Criminal, or Civil Court. Or you may go for the Employment, Coroners, Environment or Māori Land Court. The choice is yours, depending on the area of law in which you have specialised.

Our Chief Justice since 2019, Dame Helen Winkelmann, has recently spoken publicly about the way our country's judiciary is becoming more diverse. She is also adamant that today's students who graduate as lawyers can see becoming a judge as a realistic goal.[78] To that end, a Diversity Committee has been established by the Bar Association to promote more community involvement by judges, more visits to schools to inspire young students and more encouragement of law schools to diversify when selecting students.

The statistics as of 2020 are not particularly indicative of diverse ethnicities. For example, 92 per cent of students entering Otago's law school identified as being of European descent while 3 per cent at Canterbury's law school were Pasifika.[79]

In law firms, diversity is yet to become a reality. So too is law becoming a consideration for those from working-class families. But diversity on the bench is crucial if our judges are to be representative of the people.

So, think about it. Mark Twain reckoned the two most important days in your life are the day you were born and the day you find out why. Discovering your passion and acting on it is enormously fulfilling, and who knows, it may be the bench.

If after reading this, you decide that law is not for you, you could aim for a more opportunistic career and be like the parking attendant who suddenly disappeared after a decades-long career. That prompted a worried customer to enquire, 'What happened to the guy at the entrance who collected all the parking fees and even told us where the free spots are? Did he retire?'

The employee was somewhat confused.

'Madam, parking has been free ever since we opened.'

33 The after life

WHAT DO YOU DO when that job you have loved comes to an abrupt end? When you plan to ease out of it gradually but life intervenes and your plans go awry?

For every single day I was a judge, I loved the job. Sure, there were pressures, but never once did I ever consider walking away. I felt I had found my vocation and every difficult case was part of the challenge that I relished. I knew I could be a judge until I turned 70 and there was the possibility of working part-time after that.

Then Mike got cancer, completely out of the blue.

He had always been healthy and prided himself on never having spent a night in hospital.

We believed we had found our soulmate in each other, and that had helped us to navigate the storms our children experienced and the twists and turns that any couple faced. But in March 2017, the diagnosis came. Aggressive prostate cancer with a Gleason score of 10, the highest possible under that cancer-grading scheme, indicating the aggressiveness of Mike's cancer. Mike, half-jokingly, on learning the diagnosis, said, 'Well, I hear most men die with prostate cancer, rather than of it.'

'Not you my friend,' was the grave reply. This was cancer which demanded action. A prostatectomy followed to remove the offending prostate. But that was only partly successful and his successive PSA blood test scores doubled quickly, showing the cancer was still present. He then went on a hormone-reduction regime and found out what women suffer with — regular hot flushes.

The written diagnosis gave Mike 18 months to two years to live.

Our planned trip to Canada had to be abandoned and, instead, January 2018 saw us travel to Central Otago where we lived in a straw bale house, built by writer Jillian Sullivan. Our daughter Polly joined us with her dog, Lola, and for a month we experienced the idyllic vast blue skies and endless landscape of Ōtūrehua. And that's where fate intervened.

I could see the wonderful soothing effect this land had on Mike. Polly loved it just as much and decided she would sell her house and move there. We went to an art exhibition and met writers, poets and artists.

Mike felt like he had come home.

That night I lay awake and plotted and planned how we might be able to live here with me working part-time. I had been a judge then for 12 years, time spent in the Waikato because of *my* job. Now it was time to redress the balance.

I woke Mike in the morning and told him of my decision. He was completely chuffed. The next day we found the house that was for sale, which had a separate section attached, enough for Polly's new home to be built there.

We told our daughter Katherine. She and her husband decided to follow us. Our son Matthew and his wife lived in Panama City, so the decision impacted less on him.

I retired at the end of 2018 from full-time work, a hard decision, but I consoled myself I would still be able to work part-time, being sent wherever I was needed.

The best laid plans . . . That work all over the country proved to be gruelling, especially as we live nearly two hours from the nearest airport. By the end of 2019, it became apparent it was simply not viable. I stopped.

I took up Spanish lessons, so I would be able, one day, to communicate with Matt's new baby Matteo. I became enthusiastic about gardening, played my beloved baby grand piano daily and told myself it would be okay. I hoped Truman Capote was wrong when he said that life is a moderately good play with a badly written third act.

Polly had died in October 2018 and so she never got to see her new house, quaint and finished, next door to us. We invited folk to stay there to recharge their batteries and wondered what the future held for the wee house.

Then, in October 2019, we had Polly's unveiling at the local cemetery. My 91-year-old mother, by now a widow, came for the occasion, a little grudgingly as she could not understand why we had moved to 'that place', as she disparagingly called it.

During the unveiling on a cloudless windless day, we watched as Mum's panama hat came off her head and skittered and danced out of reach. A video captured it as people tried and failed to grab the errant hat. We all marvelled at how it flew; 'Polly's obviously having fun,' we said.

For Mum it held deeper significance. After the ceremony, she stood in the lounge of Polly's place and said, more to herself than anyone else, 'I could live here.' I dashed next door to check with Mike, 'Could you cope with your mother-in-law living next door?'

'Of course,' came the reply.

And so she moved, leaving family and friends in the sunny Bay of Plenty, for a wee village which boasts the lowest winter temperatures in New Zealand.

As I write, the ground is covered with snow and has been for days. A hoar frost has rendered everything glistening white. Even the spiderwebs are resplendent with ice. The temperatures have been as low as minus 12.

My mother, wrapped in her double-glazed heated house, loves it.

Polly would be laughing like a drain to think her beloved

grandmum is now living here. 'Meant to be,' she'd say.

Mike's cancer goes on.

Radiation treatment in March 2020 didn't get it all. He is now described as being in the palliative care stage with chemo happening over the next four months. Mike says the only time he feels sick is when he goes to the doctor.

We are determined, though, not to live in the shadow of cancer. He wouldn't go so far as to call it a friend, but nor does he believe he is fighting the enemy. Each day is a gift. We have each other, this beautiful Ida Valley where we live with its mountains looming over us, its impossibly big sky, and family around us.

And, too, a fine collection of writers, poets, artists and locals who have become firm friends. We instituted a writers' retreat, a weekend event for 50 people. It was a great success in September 2019. Thereafter, the plan is to hold annual week-long retreats for 20 writers to work on a particular project of their own and to provide tutors from our midst to assist them. The first of those occurred in September 2020 and the feedback confirmed we were on to something special.

Mike is turning out more books and has plans for a wildflower garden next summer. It's always good to look ahead. He has in mind his late friend Tom who, when he knew his cancer was terminal, planted over 5000 daffodils on his property. It is known as taking the long view.

And me?

Well, after six months of people saying you really should write a book about being a judge, and me saying to myself I couldn't possibly do *that*, I capitulated. One day I sat down with pen and paper and, as I wrote, the regret about giving up the job lifted. The idea I had kept batting away, telling it to bother someone else, refused to leave. When an idea keeps hovering like that and comes at you from all directions, it is time to pay attention.

Maybe there is something in the saying that when you

bring peace to your past, you can move forward to your future. For me, the peace, or at least the lifting of regret, lay in setting out this story of being a judge over 14 years, recalling all the funny and sad stories, the brave and the cowardly, the mundane and the extraordinary.

Despite the shameless enjoyment of writing, there were plenty of reasons not to write this story. Some might feel the mystique of being a judge should not be uncovered, or that judging, by its nature, is a serious business, diminished somewhat by poking the borax. Or that to write in such a light-hearted way is somehow shameful.

I haven't named names, but some might see themselves here and be offended. I also wondered, is it *appropriate* to write such a tale?

Was I being unbecoming?

But then I had two thoughts.

The first is I am 68 and I'm done with fear.

The second is how broken and scared we all are — even those that seem to have it together. Judges are only human. Maybe it is time to tell *that* story.

And so, here it is.

Notes

1   Interview, *Kiwis First: Legal News from New Zealand*, 13 March 2013.

2   'Judge breaks down at sentencing', *Stuff*, 19 November 2009.

3   *The Guardian*, 23 October 2017.

4   Edith Eger, *The Choice*, Penguin Random House UK, 2017, p. 280.

5   Anne Lamott, *Traveling Mercies: some thoughts on faith*, Pantheon Books, 1999.

6   Jodi Picoult, *Nineteen Minutes*, Atria, 2007.

7   *The Elements of Style*, Third Edition, 1979, p. 84.

8   T.S. Eliot, from 'Burnt Norton' in *Four Quartets*.

9   Dan Howell, from Goodreads.com, Quotable Quotes.

10   *Toronto Star*, 26 June 2002.

11   Scoop Independent News article, 'Anti Father Family Court Judges exposed', 23 January 2001.

12   Zombie Democracy — Apartheid Fort New Zealand article headed 'Evil Judges'.

13   Fourth Estate, Wikipedia.

14   Amy Adams, 'NZ's highest rate of family violence in the developed world — Amy Adams has "had enough"', *Stuff*, 21 March 2017.

15   New Zealand Government, *Family Violence It's Not OK*, statistics.

16   Radio NZ, *Getting Tough: how New Zealand could stop domestic violence*, 20 September 2019.

17   Cited in *Family Violence Death Review Committee Fifth Report Data*, January 2009 to December 2015.

18   Mackinac Center for Public Policy, Michigan, July 2018.

19   'Why does New Zealand imprison so many Maori?', *Frank*, 21

August 2020. Hannah McGlue, 'Addressing the imbalance: enhancing women's opportunities to build offence free lives through gender responsivity', *Practice: the New Zealand Corrections journal*, Volume 5, Issue 2, November 2017.

20 BBC News, *How Norway turns criminals into good neighbours*, 6 July 2019.

21 Malcolm Gladwell, *The Tipping Point: how little things can make a big difference*, Little, Brown, 2000, p. 7.

22 Chris Marshall, *Compassionate Justice*, Cascade Books, 2012.

23 Tadhg Daly and Matthew McClennan, *Three Strikes Law*, Ministry of Justice, December 2018.

24 I.F. Stone, *The Trial of Socrates*, Little, Brown and Company, 1988.

25 *East Anglian Times*, 18 May 2018.

26 Stephen Pile, *The Book of Heroic Failures*, Futura, 1979.

27 Katarina Williams, 'Financial hardship no reason for skipping jury duty, minister says', *Stuff*, 21 September 2017.

28 NZPA, '"Yo Judge" lawyer says in court', *Stuff*, 24 September 2009.

29 New Zealand Law Society, 'NZ Supreme Court leads in proportion of women judges', 22 June 2017.

30 Statistics New Zealand, 2 April 2019, reporting on findings for the 2017/2018 financial year.

31 Newshub, 'South Auckland loan agency using "rough" methods', 8 December 2013.

32 *New Zealand's Debt Society and Child Poverty*. Background Paper by Dr M. Claire Dale, p. 15.

33 Child Poverty Action Group (CPAG) report, 2019, p. 4.

34 Cited in *O'Neill v Toogood, Croucher and Amon* [2017] NZHC 795 at [25].

35 *Ruka v DSW*]1997] 1 NZLR 154.

36 Oralee Wachter, *No More Secrets for Me,* Little, Brown Books, 1983.

37 One Pump Court article, 28 June 2017.

38 In *K v K* (2009) NZFLR 241.

39 *Tote Investors Ltd v Smoker* (1968) QB 509.

40 *Marsden v Regan* (1954) All ER 475.

41 *Braham v J Lyons & Co Ltd* [1962] 1WLR 1048.

42 *Helton v State* 31150, 2d 381 1975. The verse was included in defence submissions.

43 *Porreco v Porreco* 811 A. 2d 566 Pa 2002 Eakin J.

44 *Lowe v Auckland City Council*, High Court 12/5/1993.

45   *Green v Green* (1989) 17 NSWLR 343 at 346.

46   *R v Sussex Justices ex p McCarthy* [1924] 1 KB 256.

47   Barbara Sumner, *Tree of Strangers*, Massey University Press, 2020.

48   Ibid., p. 226.

49   *Fitzgerald v R* [2020] NZCA 292. However, leave has been given to appeal part of the decision. It was to be heard by the Supreme Court on 23 February 2021.

50   Michelle Duff, 'The number of newborn babies removed from their parents is rising', *Stuff*, 12 December 2018.

51   *O'Neill v Toogood, Croucher and Amon* [2017] NZHC 795.

52   Hamish Hastie, '"No Prospect": Doubt cast on McGowan's "vexatious litigant" defence for Palmer lawsuit onslaught', *Sydney Morning Herald*, 28 August 2020.

53   'Meet the "vexatious litigants": people who can't stop going to court', *Longreads*, 23 July 2014.

54   *Evening Post*, 10 February 2007.

55   BBC News, 'Black barrister mistaken for defendant three times gets apology', 24 September 2020.

56   *Borell v The Queen* [2020] NZCA 235.

57   Para [42].

58   Safe and Effective Justice Advisory Group, *Turuki! Turuki! Transforming our criminal justice system.*

59   Robert Fisher QC, 'The Demeanour Fallacy', *New Zealand Law Review*, [4] p575–602.

60   Studies performed by Sheena Lyengar, Columbia University.

61   Described in digitalwellbeing.org, *The Jam Study Strikes Back: when less choice does mean more sales*, 19 January 2015, a study conducted by Sheena Lyengar and Mark Lepper.

62   *Williams v Aucutt* [2000] 2 NZLR 479 (CA), *Auckland City Mission v Brown* [2002]2 NZLR 650 (CA) and *Henry v Henry* [2007] NZCA 42.

63   Emma Lunn, 'Contested wills reach all time high in 2019', *Your Money*, 20 July 2020.

64   Zheping Huang, 'Xi Jinping promised legal reform in China but forget about judicial independence', *Quartz*, 18 January 2017.

65   K.D. Singh, 'A critical look at the 2002 Re: Arundhati Roy decision and modern-day contempt laws', *Legally India*, 30 March 2015.

66   Ibid.

67   Justice Michael Kirby, *Attacks on Judges — A Universal Phenomenon*, American Bar Association Section of Litigation Winter Leadership Meeting, Maui, Hawaii, 5 January 1998.

68 sluggerotoole.com, 26 January 2012.

69 E.G. Hall, 'Contempt of court and the legal profession', *Gazette of the Law Society of Ireland*, Volume 94, 2000, pp. 12–15.

70 'Law Society says no further action against Catriona MacLennan for criticising judge', *New Zealand Herald*, 15 May 2018.

71 New Zealand Bar Association Press Release, 'Politicians urged to be cautious in criticising judges', *Scoop,* 21 June 2019.

72 Faizan Mustafa, 'Contempt jurisdiction should be used sparingly', *The Tribune*, 18 March 2019.

73 Ministry of Health figures.

74 This account of a young graduate is taken from the New Zealand Foundation website in one of their articles from Volume 25, Issue Number 4, November 2014.

75 Nick Butcher, 'The Right Track', *Law Talk*, Issue 928, 10 May 2019.

76 Nikki Macdonald, 'Talent-spotted while waitressing, Tiana Epati now leads the law profession', *Stuff,* 20 April 2019.

77 Elizabeth Gilbert, *Big Magic: creative living beyond fear*, Free Press, 1989.

78 Stephen R. Covey, *The Seven Habits of Highly Effective People*, Bloomsbury Publishing, 2015.

79 Mike White, 'Diversity badly lacking among New Zealand's judges', *Stuff,* 4 October 2020.

80 LawFuel editors, 'The gender & ethnic diversity issue with New Zealand's law profession', *LawFuel*, 4 October 2020.

Acknowledgments

I'M SURE NO BOOK is written without a number of cheerleaders and supporters waving their flags on the sidelines. My team have been fantastic and a great big thank you is due to a number of people who believed in me and prodded me on when life seemed gloomy in lockdown and I couldn't find a way out or beyond that of being a judge. Write a book they said!

In our village thanks must go to friends and fellow writers Brian Turner, Jillian Sullivan, Bridget Auchmuty and Paula Wagemaker, to Stefan Jahn a visitor from Germany who read the first draft and provided comments from a non-native English speaker, and further afield in Otago to Alan Coull and Michael Harlow who kept asking when I was going to write that book.

I contacted a few judges during the writing process and they happily provided their own stories. Thanks to Judges Annis Somerville, Peter Rollo, Geoff Rea, Jenny Binns, Paul Geoghegan, Jocelyn Munro, Lee Spear and Chris McGuire. I may have tweaked your stories somewhat in the interests of decorum, but your reminiscences reminded me again what an extraordinary career we have all had.

All judges would agree that court staff do a fantastic job under sometimes trying circumstances. Dealing with the public can have its challenges, especially when people are in an unwelcome environment, feeling stressed or emotional. I want to single out the court staff at Hamilton, Morrinsville, Huntly and Gisborne for special mention. You know who you are. You are all stars.

To Pat Dunmore, Kevin Chapman and Warren Adler at Upstart Press, thank you for making the publishing process so seamless and for believing in this book.

To my mother Lorna Scott, married for 61 years to a writer she prodded as mercilessly as she did me, thank you. Your fierce determination is something you have passed on to all your children.

Katherine and Chas live just down the road and we see them every day. To have one's daughter and son-in-law so close is a real blessing. They are both so incredibly supportive and loving. Katherine typed up my first stab at putting pen to paper and her hoots of laughter convinced me that maybe I was on to something.

Matthew and his wife Maru and son Matteo live in Panama City. Matthew's creativity in the computer arena is boundless. He believes there is always a solution and his enthusiasm is infectious, especially to an aspiring writer.

Polly would have loved this story. She inherited her father's raucous laugh and I have heard her more than once during the writing process. She was always a great believer in me and her steady flow of cards and notes, still dripping glitter, are a constant reminder of her love.

But it all comes back to Mike who has stood by me since our inauspicious beginnings in a flat in Stoke Newington, London. He appeared in the doorway one day with his brother Kevin looking for somewhere to stay. I managed the money for the flat of 12 or more and was in the middle of a rant about people who weren't paying their five pounds a week rent.

'And if you don't pay your share you'll be out too', as I rounded on him. He said it was love at first sight.

Since that day early in January 1974, Mike has been part

of everything I've achieved, all the while becoming the kind of writer I could only dream about. He may have described himself as a judge's handbag in recent years, but that does not do justice to his unwavering love and commitment. He stands beside me, nudging, challenging and believing in me. And that is why this book is dedicated to him.

About the author

ROSEMARY RIDDELL is the daughter of Scots immigrants to Aotearoa New Zealand. They instilled in her their virtues of hard work, determination and indomitable endurance. With her own adventurous streak, she took to finding her place in the world with persistence and pizzaz.

Her beginnings in broadcasting and theatre took her to Europe, where fame and fortune didn't eventuate, but she did find a life partner with whom she returned to her homeland and raised three children. Her love of acting morphed into a law degree at Auckland University and a subsequent career in legal practice.

Eventually washing up as a partner in a Dunedin firm, her creative drive managed to find expression alongside the formal vocation. She directed a short film, *Cake Tin*, which won an award in Hollywood, and acted in and directed the play *Jerusalem, Jersualem* — touring it around New Zealand and to the Edinburgh Fringe Festival.

Stimulated by the experience, Rosemary directed the award-winning feature film *The Insatiable Moon*. Alongside all of this she kept up her legal work, eventually being appointed as a judge of the District Court in 2006, and she served in the Hamilton Court until retirement. She now lives in Central Otago, where her interests include piano, gardening, reading, and writing books.